ALL OF US NEED A PLACE OF OUR ̵̵̵̵̵
A HOUSE TO CALL, "HOME SWEET HOME."

BIRDS HAVE A NEST AND BEARS HAVE A DEN,
THERE'S A BARN FOR THE COW, A COOP FOR THE HEN.

A WEB FOR THE SPIDER AND STREAMS FOR THE FISH,
AND LIONS MAY LIVE WHEREVER THEY WISH!

THE HEAVENLY ANGELS HAVE SKIES ABOVE,
FROM WHICH TO SPRINKLE A MAGICAL LOVE.

THERE MUST BE A WAY TO KEEP THEM HERE,
TO JOYOUSLY SPREAD THEIR WARMTH AND CHEER.

BUILD THEM A PLACE ALL OF THEIR OWN —
AN ANGEL HOUSE, A "HOME SWEET HOME."

THE PLANS ARE SIMPLE. THE WAY IS TRUE.
TO SAY TO THE ANGELS, "I LOVE YOU!"

ANGEL
HOMES

CREATE A SPECIAL PLACE
FOR AN ANGEL

ANGEL HOMES

CREATE A SPECIAL PLACE FOR AN ANGEL

VANESSA-ANN

Sterling Publishing Co., Inc.   New York

A Sterling / Chapelle Book

Chapelle:

- Jo Packham, Owner
- Cathy Sexton, Editor
- Pauline Locke, Artist
- Staff: Malissa Boatwright, Kass Burchett, Rebecca Christensen, Marilyn Goff, Michael Hannah, Shirley Heslop, Holly Hollingsworth, Susan Jorgensen, Ginger Mikkelsen, Barbara Milburn, Linda Orton, Karmen Quinney, Leslie Ridenour, and Cindy Stoeckl

Designers:

- Holly Fuller • Kelly Hendersen • Susan Laws • Cindy Rooks

Photography:

- Kevin Dilley, Photographer for Hazen Photography
- Susan Laws, Photo Stylist for Chapelle

If you have any questions or comments or would like information on specialty products featured in this book, please contact Chapelle, Ltd., Inc., P.O. Box 9252, Ogden, UT 84409 • (801) 621-2777 • (801) 621-2788 Fax

Due to the limited amount of space available, we must print our patterns at a reduced size in order to give our patrons the maximum number of patterns possible in our publications. We believe the quality and quantity of our patterns will compensate for any inconvenience this may cause.

Library of Congress Cataloging-in-Publication Data

Angel homes : create a special place for an angel / Vanessa-Ann.
            p.   cm.
        "A Sterling / Chapelle book."
        Includes index.
        ISBN 0-8069-9769-9
        1. Woodwork--Patterns. 2. Painted woodwork. 3. Dollhouses.
        4. Dwellings in art. I. Vanessa-Ann Collection (Firm)
        TT200.A53 1997
        684'.08--dc21
                                                97-22146
                                                CIP

10 9 8 7 6 5 4 3 2 1

Published by Sterling Publishing Company, Inc.
387 Park Avenue South, New York, NY 10016
© 1997 by Chapelle Ltd.
Distributed in Canada by Sterling Publishing
c/o Canadian Manda Group, One Atlantic Avenue, Suite 105
Toronto, Ontario, Canada M6K 3E7
Distributed in Great Britain and Europe by Cassell PLC
Wellington House, 125 Strand, London WC2R 0BB, England
Distributed in Australia by Capricorn Link (Australia) Pty Ltd.
P.O. Box 6651, Baulkham Hills, Business Centre, NSW 2153, Australia
Printed in Hong Kong
All Rights Reserved

Sterling ISBN 0-8069-9769-9

NOW I LAY ME DOWN TO SLEEP,
I PRAY THE LORD MY SOUL TO KEEP.
BUT WHAT ABOUT MY ANGEL DEAR,
WHO SMOOTHS THE WAY AND CALMS MY FEAR?

WHERE WILL SHE LAY HER HEAD TONIGHT,
TO REST HER WINGS FROM WEARY FLIGHT?
ON A STARDUST PILLOW AND A CLOUD SOFT BED,
IN A PRECIOUS LITTLE HOUSE WHERE
GOD'S LOVE IS SHED.

IN HER OWN ANGEL HOUSE,
WITH ITS LIGHT SHINING BRIGHT.
GOOD NIGHT, SWEET ANGEL,
GOOD NIGHT, SLEEP TIGHT.

CONTENTS

GENERAL INSTRUCTIONS

GENERAL TOOLS & ADHESIVES

- Table saw
- Jigsaw
- Miter saw
- Drill and drill bit
- Sandpaper
- Tack cloth
- Graphite paper
- Stylus
- Ruler
- Pencil
- Craft knife
- Pliers
- Toothpick
- Paintbrushes
- Lining brushes
- Sponge
- Plastic wrap
- Masking tape
- Dremel tool
- Fabric scissors
- Craft scissors
- Needles
- Wood filler
- Wood glue
- Industrial-strength glue
- Craft glue
- Hot glue gun and glue sticks
- Découpage glue
- Rubber cement

SELECTING WOODS

Two types of wood were used for the construction of the angel houses featured in this book. The $1/4$"-thick wood used is birch plywood. The $1/2$"-thick wood used is pine.

Both of these types of woods are common woods that are durable, readily available, and easy to use.

Other types of woods can be used for the construction of these angel houses, but additional prep time might be necessary depending upon the grade quality of the chosen wood(s).

Balsa wood has been used on many of the angel houses for doors, porch posts and/or supports, window boxes, and shutters.

Because it is an extremely lightweight wood, it can easily be cut with a sharp craft knife. This makes the perfect wood choice for these types of applications.

CUTTING WOODS

When cutting the birch plywood and the pine into appropriate shapes according to the angel house blueprints, the dimensions given are width x height.

A table saw is recommended for cutting these pieces because a table saw can accommodate large pieces of wood.

However, other saws can be used depending on the skill of the wood cutter.

In all instances, electric saws are dangerous power tools and all precautions should be taken when using them. Goggles must be worn at all times for eye protection.

The jigsaw is used for every project to cut out windows and doors. Drilling a pilot hole first will allow the jigsaw blade to get into the area and the cut should be made following all transferred lines.

TRANSFERRING WINDOWS & DOORS

The first step in transferring windows and doors is to determine exactly where they should be placed.

There are basically three methods to arrive at these calculations.

The first method is to simply enlarge the patterns according to the percentages given. Once the enlargements have been made, the windows and doors should be in the correct positions. Next, tape the pattern onto the wood and, using graphite paper and a stylus, trace around the windows and doors until they are accurately transferred to the wood.

The second method is to mathematically calculate the positions. Since all outside dimensions have been provided, along with all window and door dimensions, the calculations can be determined using a graphing calculator.

The third method is to use personal judgement by placing windows and doors as desired.

The actual transferring should be done using graphite paper and a stylus.

CUTTING WINDOWS & DOORS

Once windows and doors have been transferred to the wood, they are ready to be cut out.

If the window (or door) is positioned inside the dimensions of the piece of wood and cannot be accessed by cutting from an outside edge, a drill and $1/4"$ drill bit should be used to drill pilot holes in each corner of the windows (and door). This enables the crafter to get a jigsaw into the wood to make the necessary cuts.

A jigsaw is the best tool to use to cut out the windows and doors because a jigsaw can easily be used when cutting in small areas.

SANDING WOODS

A little sanding will always be necessary. It is recommended that a medium-grit sandpaper be used for sanding rough edges.

Additional sanding might be necessary when wood filler is used.

ASSEMBLING ANGEL HOUSES

The basic components for each angel house have been named and color coded for the crafter's ease in determining which pieces are which.

For example, all fronts are pink, all backs are lavander, all sides are blue, all bases are green, all roofs are yellow, and all walls and chimneys are peach. Refer to the photograph on top of page 9.

In the materials list for each angel house, the colors are given again as an additional check. In addition, whenever a piece has been altered from its original dimensions, an asterisk (*) has been placed in the materials list to alert the crafter of the change.

Begin the assembly process by placing the fronts and the backs parallel to each other.

Using wood glue, glue one side (pitched piece in most cases) to each end of fronts and backs, aligning all outside edges. Do not glue pitched pieces "inside" fronts and backs, as this will not allow the roofs to fit properly on top of the angel houses.

Refer to the photograph below and make certain all sides are glued on the outside of the fronts and backs.

Finally, allow glue to dry thoroughly after each step.

Once the fronts, backs, and sides have been glued together and the glue has been allowed to thoroughly dry, the assembled angel house can then be glued to the base.

Align the bases according to the individual instructions for the angel houses.

Refer to the photograph at top of page 10. Allow glue to dry thoroughly.

Do not glue the roofs on until instructed to do so. All of the angel houses require some access to the inside from the top to secure windows, doors and door frames, curtains, and embellishments and this cannot be done once the roofs have been glued into position.

The roof pieces should be glued together and the glue allowed to dry. Once the glue is thoroughly dry, the roofs are ready to be glued onto the angel houses, but do not do so until instructed.

If the angle of the roof is 45°, the dimensions of the roof pieces will vary only by the width of the wood being used ($^1/_4$" or $^1/_2$").

The smaller of the two pieces of wood should "butt" up against the outside long edge of the larger piece, thus making the appropriate 45° angle.

If the angle of the roof is anything other than 45°, the dimensions of the roof pieces will be identical. When this occurs, one long end of each roof piece will need to be mitered to fit together properly.

The angle that these long ends should be mitered is the same as the angle of the roof.

Refer to the photographs on this page. Allow glue to dry thoroughly.

When instructed, glue assembled roof to top of angel house.

Refer to the photograph on page 11. Allow glue to dry thoroughly.

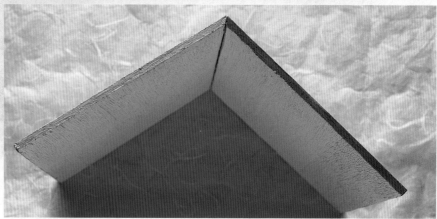

BASE COATING:

Base coating is the technique that is used to do most of the painting on the angel houses featured in this book.

It is the application of acrylic paint to all painting surfaces for full, opaque coverage. The painting surfaces should be covered with two to three smooth, even coats of paint.

It is better to apply several thin coats of paint rather than one heavy coat. Allow paint to dry thoroughly between coats.

If the paint causes the wood grain to raise, lightly sand the rough surfaces before applying additional coats of paint.

DRY BRUSHING:

Dry brushing is done by loading a paintbrush with a small amount of acrylic paint.

The excess paint in the paintbrush is then wiped on a paper towel until there is very little paint left in the bristles.

The paintbrush is then held in a vertical position and the paint is applied in a circular motion moving from the center to the outside. The color will soften toward the outer edges.

INSTALLING HARDWARE

When hinge assemblies are necessary for hanging doors (or shutters), it can seem almost impossible to work with such small pieces of hardware.

A dremel tool is a small power tool that is perfect for these types of applications. Because the drill bits on a dremel are so small, they aid in providing pilot holes for the screws to install the appropriate hardware.

TRANSFERRING SAYINGS

Transferring sayings onto wood should be done using graphite paper and a stylus.

Oftentimes it is easiest to transfer sayings onto the appropriate wood piece before that piece has been assembled. For example, if the saying goes on the roof, transferring it while the roof is a single piece of wood is easiest. However, if the roof piece has not been painted, the transferring cannot be done until it has been painted.

WASHING:

This technique refers to the application of acrylic paint to a surface for transparent coverage. It is done by mixing the paint with water in a 1:3 ratio (25% paint to 75% water).

Thinned paint should never be applied to unsealed wood.

Apply several coats to produce a soft, but deep, transparent color.

DECORATING ANGEL HOUSES ON THE INSIDE

Once the angel house has been assembled, but before the roof has been glued into position, the inside of the angel house can be decorated.

Be careful not to get too extravagent, because in most cases very little of the inside will actually show. However, every angel house should have those special touches that transform it from a house into a home.

The inside walls can be painted or wallpapered with wallpaper or fabric that has adhesive on one side. Paint, carpet, wallpaper, fabric, and/or small tiles can be placed on the floor.

If pictures are hung on the walls or furniture is added inside, they must be glued in place so they cannot shift once angel house has been completed.

ADDING LIGHTS ON THE INSIDE

Small strands of electrical lights can be added so each angel house can be illuminated when desired.

Lights can simply be added around the perimeter of the roof and/or windows similar to hanging Christmas lights around a house. This adds a festive touch to angel houses that have a holiday theme.

If it is desired to have lights on the inside of the angel house for illumination, a notch, similar to the once shown in the photograph below, must be cut in the base to accommodate the electrical cords.

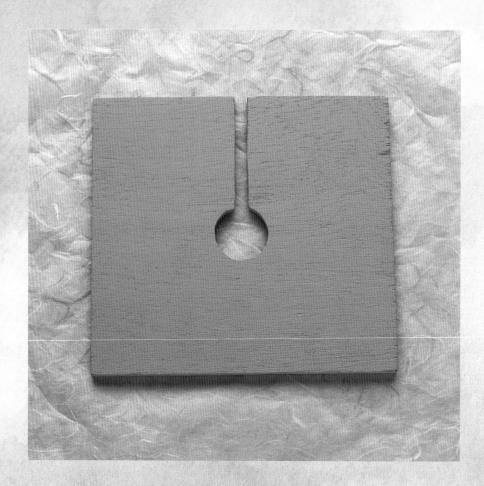

the rock loft

materials

Wood:
- ☐ Front, $5^1/_2$" x $3^5/_8$" x $^1/_4$"
- ☐ Back, $5^1/_2$" x $3^5/_8$" x $^1/_4$"
- ☐ Sides, $6^1/_4$" x $6^3/_4$" x $^1/_4$" (2)
- ☐ Base, 6" x $6^1/_4$" x $^1/_4$"
- ☐ Roof, $7^1/_2$" x $4^3/_4$" x $^1/_4$"
- ☐ Roof, $7^1/_2$" x 5" x $^1/_4$"
- ☐ Chimney, $2^1/_4$" x 6" x 2"

Balsa wood:
$^1/_8$" x $^3/_8$" x 20"

Windows & door, $^1/_{24}$ scale:
Windows, $2^{25}/_{32}$" x $1^9/_{32}$" (2)
Cotton lace,
 1"-wide x $^1/_4$ yard

Hardware, $^1/_{24}$ scale:
Door hinge assemblies (2)
Door knob

Siding:
Clapboard siding, $^1/_2$"
 (3 sheets)

Decorative accessories:
Flat rocks,
 $^1/_2$" to $1^1/_2$" long
Sanded tile grout, white
Plastic wrap
Masking tape

Embellishments, optional:
Large flat rock

Paints & finishes:
Brown, dark brown,
 dark gray, off-white,
 and tan acrylic paints
Antiquing medium
Texturizing gel
Liquid varnish
Satin acrylic spray

how-to

1. Before beginning, carefully read General Instructions on pages 7-12.

2. Note: This angel house has been rotated so the front and back become the sides and the sides become the front and back.

3. Using a table saw, cut wood for front, back, sides, base, and roof using basic studio blueprints on page 114.

4. Cut wood for chimney using the studio chimney pattern on page 122.

5. Using graphite paper and a stylus, transfer windows on front and one side and door on front using window and door placement patterns on page 17.

6. Using a drill and $^1/_4$" drill bit, drill pilot holes in each corner of windows, including windows on front door.

7. Using a jigsaw, cut out windows and door. Save and set door aside.

8. Cut window openings in door using door pattern on page 17.

On the roof of the angel house: *angels in this home are blessed within these walls of peace and rest.*

17. Float-shade under each row of shingles with dark brown.

18. Apply antiquing medium to all painted pieces, except window frames, according to manufacturer's directions.

19. Using a toothpick, apply wood glue around window frames and set them in place.

20. Apply texturizing gel to chimney according to manufacturer's directions. Texturizing gel should not be placed on chimney where roof is to be positioned.

21. Use texturizing gel to build up an edge around top perimeter of chimney.

22. Using a paintbrush, paint chimney with off-white acrylic paint, then lightly dry-brush with dark brown, brown, and tan acrylic paints.

23. Paint inside built up edge around top perimeter of chimney with dark gray acrylic paint.

24. Using wood glue, attach chimney to side of angel house using notch placement pattern on page 17.

9. Cut a 2¹/₄"-wide x ³/₈" high notch centered along 7¹/₂" edge of 4³/₄" roof to accommodate chimney using notch placement pattern on page 17.

10. Using wood glue, assemble front, back, and sides of angel house. <u>Note: Do not glue roof on at this time.</u>

11. Glue assembled angel house on base, aligning front, back, and sides with outside edges of base.

12. Glue clapboard siding to roof for shingles.

13. Using a paintbrush, paint angel house on the inside with off-white acrylic paint.

14. Paint both sides of roof, including all outside edges, with off-white.

15. Paint both sides of window frames and a ¹/₂" border around cut out for door on front of angel house with off-white.

16. Paint both sides of door and ¹/₈"-thick balsa wood for roof trim with dark brown acrylic paint.

25. Using craft glue, randomly place and adhere flat rocks to front, back, and sides of angel house using photograph on page 13 for placement. Rocks should not be placed on upper edges of angel house where roof is to be positioned.

26. Using a hot glue gun and glue sticks, make a bead of hot glue around each rock to secure the rock in place while craft glue dries.

27. Mix sanded tile grout according to manufacturer's directions.

28. Mask area around chimney with plastic wrap and masking tape.

29. Apply sanded tile grout around rocks, removing excess tile grout.

30. Remove plastic wrap and masking tape.

31. Using a dremel tool, carefully attach door to front of angel house with door hinge assemblies.

32. Using industrial-strength glue, attach door knob to front side of door.

33. Using fabric scissors, cut lace into two 4½" pieces.

34. Using industrial-strength glue, attach lace to windows on inside of angel house to make curtains.

35. Using wood glue, attach roof on angel house.

36. Using a craft knife, cut ⅛"-thick balsa wood to fit pitch of roof in front and in back of angel house and glue in place.

37. Using graphite paper and a stylus, transfer saying below to angel house using photograph for placement.

38. Using a lining brush, paint saying with off-white acrylic paint.

39. Using a paintbrush, paint each rock with liquid varnish.

40. Seal angel house with satin acrylic spray.

41. If desired, sit angel house on a large flat rock to display.

Enlarge saying 115%

angels in this home are blessed within these walls of peace and rest.

WINDOW AND DOOR PLACEMENT PATTERNS

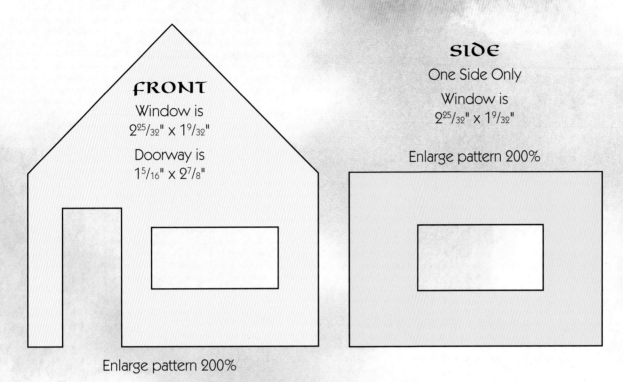

FRONT

Window is
2²⁵/₃₂" x 1⁹/₃₂"

Doorway is
1⁵/₁₆" x 2⁷/₈"

Enlarge pattern 200%

SIDE

One Side Only

Window is
2²⁵/₃₂" x 1⁹/₃₂"

Enlarge pattern 200%

NOTCH PLACEMENT PATTERN

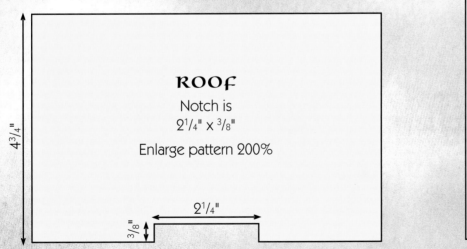

ROOF

Notch is
2¹/₄" x ³/₈"

Enlarge pattern 200%

4³/₄"

2¹/₄"

³/₈"

DOOR

Windows are
1¹/₁₆" x ¹⁵/₃₂"

Doorway is
1⁵/₁₆" x 2⁷/₈"

Pattern actual size

DOOR PATTERN

ark of angels

materials

Weathered wood:
- ☐ Front, 5¹/₂" x 3⁵/₈" x ¹/₄"
- ☐ Back, 5¹/₂" x 3⁵/₈" x ¹/₄"
- ☐ Sides, 6¹/₄" x 6³/₄" x ¹/₄" (2)
- ☐ Base, 8" x 14¹/₄" x ¹/₂" (*)
- ☐ Ark Walls,
  4¹/₂" x 14¹/₄" x ¹/₂" (2)
- ☐ Ark Walls, 5" x 7¹/₈" x ¹/₂" (2)

Hardware, ¹/₂₄ scale:
Door hinge assemblies (2)
Door handle

Decorative accessories:
Rust/brown
  chicken wire ribbon,
  3¹/₂"-wide x 1³/₈ yards
Tooling copper, 36-gauge,
  10¹/₂" x 8¹/₂"

Embellishments, optional:
Animal figurines

Paints & finishes:
Black, dark brown,
  burnt sienna, and
  dark gray acrylic paints
Copper and green patina
Top soil, dried
Matte acrylic spray

how-to

1. <u>Before beginning, care-fully read General Instructions on pages 7-12.</u>

2. <u>Note: This angel house has been rotated so the front and back become the sides and the sides become the front and back.</u>

3. Using a table saw, cut weathered wood for front, back, and sides using basic studio blueprints on page 114.

4. Cut weathered wood for base using altered dimensions given.

5. Cut weathered wood for all four ark walls using ark patterns on page 22.

6. Using a miter saw, miter each 14¹/₄" ark wall from top to bottom at a 10° angle.

7. Using graphite paper and a stylus, transfer windows on front and back and door on front using window and

door placement patterns on page 21.

8. Using a drill and ¼" drill bit, drill pilot holes in each corner of windows.

9. Using a jigsaw, cut out windows and door. Save and set door aside.

10. Using wood glue, assemble front, back, and sides

of angel house. <u>Note: Angel house roof will be made from tooling copper.</u>

11. Assemble front, back, and sides of ark. Glue angel house base on top of assembled ark. <u>Note: Do not glue angel house onto base at this time.</u>

12. Using a dremel tool, carefully attach door to front of

angel house with door hinge assemblies.

13. Using industrial-strength glue, attach door handle to front side of door.

14. Wash over hinges and door handle with dark gray acrylic paint.

15. Crinkle tooling copper with gloved hands. Flatten it

Enlarge saying 130%

It's raining, it's pouring, the thunder is roaring! As two by two the animals appear, Seeking the Angels to calm their fear.

back out by stepping on it. Slightly bend the 10$\frac{1}{2}$" sides to make pitch of roof.

16. Using a hammer and nails, center and attach roof to top of angel house.

17. Paint roof with copper patina. When thoroughly dry, apply a coat of green patina over copper patina.

18. Using wood glue, glue angel house centered on top of base.

19. Using a staple gun and staples, attach chicken wire ribbon around upper portion of ark, extending 1$\frac{3}{4}$" upward above base of angel house.

20. Paint staples with dark brown and burnt sienna acrylic paints to camouflage them on chicken wire ribbon.

21. Gently rub dried top soil over all wood surfaces for a rustic appearance. Remove excess dirt.

22. Using graphite paper and a stylus, transfer saying on page 20 to one side of ark using photograph for placement.

23. Using a lining brush, paint saying with black acrylic paint.

24. Seal angel house and ark with matte acrylic spray.

WINDOW AND DOOR PLACEMENT PATTERNS

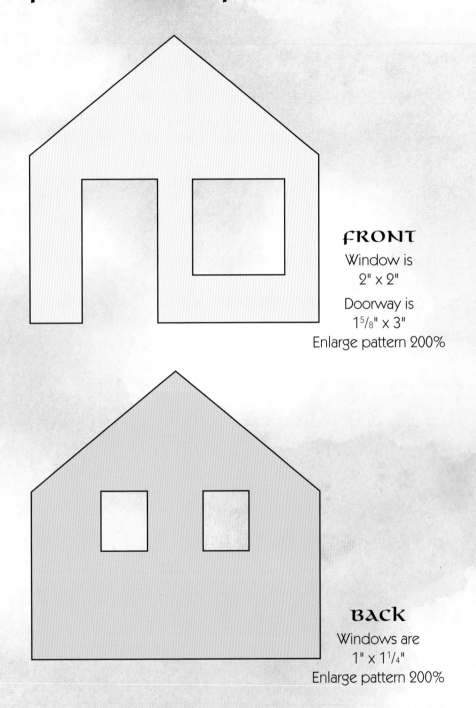

FRONT
Window is
2" x 2"
Doorway is
1$\frac{5}{8}$" x 3"
Enlarge pattern 200%

BACK
Windows are
1" x 1$\frac{1}{4}$"
Enlarge pattern 200%

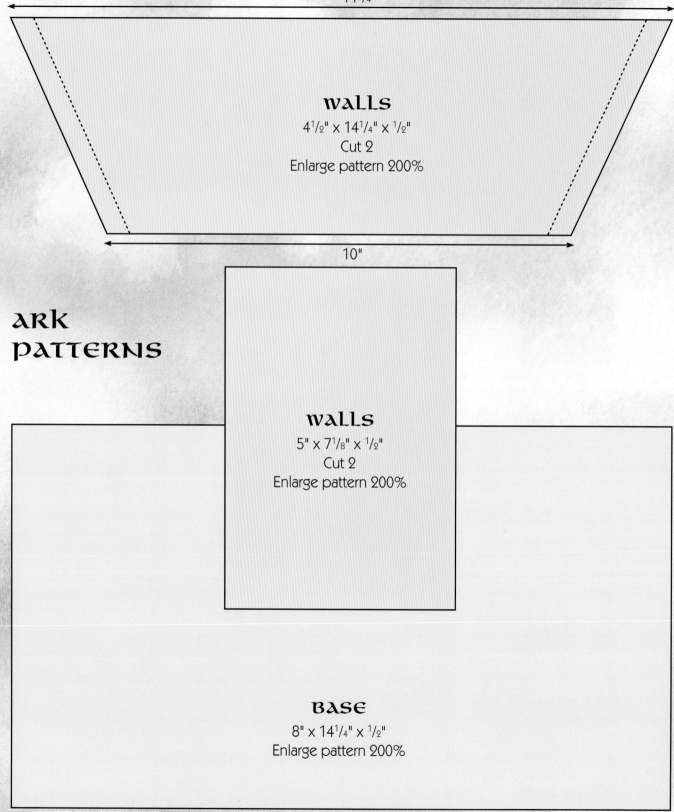

WALLS
$4^{1}/_{2}$" x $14^{1}/_{4}$" x $^{1}/_{2}$"
Cut 2
Enlarge pattern 200%

14$^{1}/_{4}$"

10"

ARK
PATTERNS

WALLS
5" x $7^{1}/_{8}$" x $^{1}/_{2}$"
Cut 2
Enlarge pattern 200%

BASE
8" x $14^{1}/_{4}$" x $^{1}/_{2}$"
Enlarge pattern 200%

home sweet home

home sweet home

MATERIALS FOR STAND

Wood:
Top of stand, 3" x 3" x 1"
Wooden dowel,
  1½"-diameter x 3' long
Base, 5" x 5" x 2"
Base, 10" x 10" x 2"

Hardware:
Wood screws, 1" (4)
Wood screw, 3" (4)

Paints & finishes:
Black acrylic paint
Matte acrylic spray

HOW-TO

1. Using a table saw, cut wood for top of stand and base using dimensions given.

2. Using wood glue, attach 5" x 5" x 2" base to top center of 10" x 10" x 2" base.

3. Using a drill and 1½" drill bit, drill a 3½" deep hole into center of assembled base of stand. Using the same drill bit, drill a ½" deep hole into the center bottom on top of stand.

4. Place wooden dowel in hole in bottom of top of stand and, using industrial-strength glue, adhere it in place. Secure in place with two 3" wood screws screwed in from top of stand down through wooden dowel.

5. Place wooden dowel in hole on top of stand base and glue it in place. Using a drill, secure it in place with two 3" wood screws screwed in from bottom of base.

6. Using a paintbrush, paint stand with black acrylic paint.

7. Seal angel house stand with matte acrylic spray.

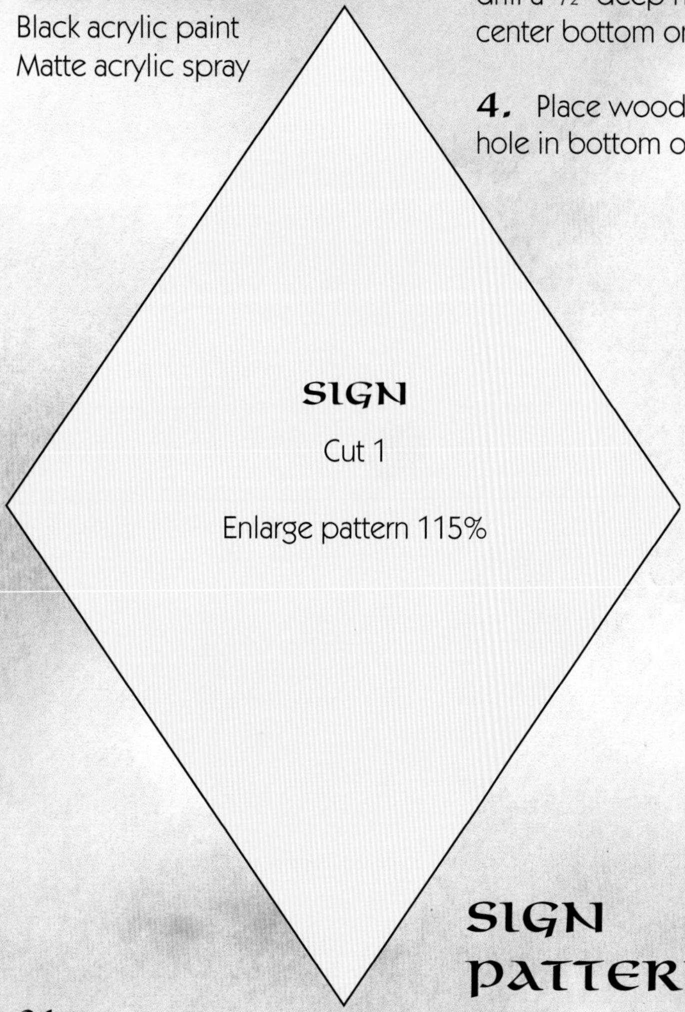

Saying actual size

In these walls so humble and small Live the Angels who care for all.

SIGN

Cut 1

Enlarge pattern 115%

SIGN PATTERN

MATERIALS FOR BOTTOM APARTMENT

Wood:
- [ ] Front, 5½" x 3⅝" x ¼"
- [ ] Back, 5½" x 3⅝" x ¼"
- [ ] Sides, 6¼" x 6¾" x ¼" (2)
- [ ] Base, 6" x 6¼" x ¼"
- [ ] Roof, 7½" x 4¾" x ¼"
- [ ] Roof, 7½" x 5" x ¼"

Balsa wood:
¼" x 5" x 7"

Hardware, ¹⁄₂₄ scale:
Door hinge assemblies (2)
Door knob
Eye screws, ¼" (4)
Chains, 1½" (2)

Decorative accessories:
Newspaper
Spool of metallic gold thread
Gold-tone leaf charms (11)

Paints & finishes:
Black, light green, light
   yellow, and metallic gold
   acrylic paints
Burnt sienna oil paint
Paint thinner
Gesso
Matte acrylic spray

HOW-TO

1. Before beginning, care-fully read General Instructions on pages 7-12.

2. Note: This angel house has been rotated so the front and back become the sides and the sides become the front and back.

3. Using a table saw, cut wood for front, back, sides, base, and roof using basic studio blueprints on page 114.

4. Lay angel house base face down on a flat surface. Turn assembled stand upside-down and center on top of angel house base. Using a drill and ¼" drill bit, drill pilot holes ½" in from each corner on top of stand.

5. Using graphite paper and a stylus, transfer windows on front and sides and door on front using window and door placement patterns on page 30.

6. Using a drill and ¼" drill bit, drill pilot holes in each corner of windows.

7. Using a jigsaw, cut out windows and door. Save and set door aside.

8. Using a craft knife, cut ¼"-thick balsa wood piece into sign using sign pattern on page 24.

9. Using wood glue, assem-ble front, back, and sides of angel house. Note: Do not glue roof on at this time.

10. Glue assembled angel house on base, aligning front, back, and sides with outside edges of base.

11. Using a paintbrush, paint angel house and base, including all outside edges, with gesso.

12. Paint both sides of angel house roof with gesso.

13. Using a paintbrush, paint angel house on the inside with light green acrylic paint, then dry-brush with light yellow acrylic paint.

14. Mix metallic gold acrylic paint and burnt sienna oil paint together and paint one side of angel house roof, both sides of door, and one side of sign. Apply paint using a swirling movement.

15. Repeat process with metallic gold acrylic paint that has not been mixed with any other color.

16. Using a lining brush, paint thin accent lines on one side of roof and door with black acrylic paint that has been thinned with water.

17. Paint thin accent lines on one side of roof and door with burnt sienna oil paint that has been thinned with paint thinner.

18. Tear the newspaper into thin strips.

19. Using découpage glue, découpage newspaper strips onto angel house according to manufacturer's directions.

20. Using a paintbrush, paint inside edges of each window and door with black acrylic paint.

21. Paint a ¼" border around each window and door with black.

22. Paint unpainted side of roof and sign, including all outside edges, with black.

23. Paint bottom of base with black.

24. Using découpage glue, découpage metallic gold thread over newspaper using photograph on page 23 for placement.

25. Using a dremel tool, carefully attach door to front of angel house with door hinge assemblies.

26. Using industrial-strength glue, attach door knob to front side of door.

27. Glue leaf charms to front of angel house using photograph for placement.

28. Place angel house on top of stand, lining up drilled pilot holes. Using 1" wood screws and a screwdriver, attach angel house to stand through pilot holes.

29. Using wood glue, attach roof on angel house.

30. Using graphite paper and a stylus, transfer saying on page 24 to sign using photograph for placement.

31. Using a lining brush, paint saying with black acrylic paint.

32. Attach eye screws to top sides of sign and to bottom corner of angel house for hanging using photograph for placement.

33. Attach chains to eye screws and position sign so it hangs appropriately.

34. Using a paintbrush, paint eye screws and chains with black.

35. Seal angel house and sign with matte acrylic spray.

MATERIALS FOR MIDDLE APARTMENT

Wood:
☐ Front, 5½" x 3⅝" x ¼"
☐ Back, 5½" x 3⅝" x ¼"
☐ Sides, 6¼" x 6¾" x ¼" (2)
☐ Base, 5¾" x 1¾" x ¼" (2) (*)
☐ Roof, 7½" x 4¾" x ¼"
☐ Roof, 7½" x 5" x ¼"

Hardware, ¹⁄₂₄ scale:
Door hinge assemblies (2)
Door knob

Decorative accessories:
Clay patio bricks,
 ⅜" square (36)
Gold-tone moon charm

Paints & finishes:
Black, dark green, light green,
 metallic gold, pink, and
 terra cotta acrylic paints
Gesso
Matte acrylic spray

HOW-TO

1. Before beginning, carefully read General Instructions on pages 7-12.

2. Note: This angel house has been rotated so the front and back become the sides and the sides become the front and back.

3. Using a table saw, cut wood for front, back, sides, and roof using basic studio blueprints on page 114.

4. Cut wood for base using altered dimensions given.

5. Using graphite paper and a stylus, transfer windows on front and sides and door on front using window and door placement patterns on page 30. Transfer inverted "V's" on sides using notch placement pattern on page 30.

6. Using a drill and ¼" drill bit, drill pilot holes in each corner of windows.

7. Using a jigsaw, cut out windows and door. Save and set door aside. Cut out "V's" on sides.

8. Using wood glue, assemble front, back, and sides of angel house. Note: Do not glue roof on at this time.

9. Glue base pieces inside assembled angel house, aligning front, back, and sides with inside edges of base. Bottoms must be flush.

10. Using a paintbrush, paint angel house and base with gesso.

11. Paint both sides of angel house roof with gesso.

12. Using a paintbrush, paint angel house on the inside with metallic gold acrylic paint.

13. Paint both sides of angel house roof, including all outside edges, with light green acrylic paint.

14. Paint both sides of door with black acrylic paint.

15. Using a lining brush, paint thin accent lines on one side of roof with dark green acrylic paint that has been thinned with water.

16. Paint thin accent lines on one side of roof with pink acrylic paint that has been thinned with water.

17. Using a sponge, sponge-paint one side of roof with dark green and pink that has been thinned with water.

18. Using a paintbrush, paint angel house with terra cotta acrylic paint.

19. Paint inside edges of each window and door with metallic gold.

20. Paint a $1/16$" border around each window and door with metallic gold.

21. Paint a $1/4$" border around each metallic gold border with black.

22. Paint bottom of base with terra cotta.

23. Paint 18 clay patio bricks with terra cotta and remaining 18 with black.

24. Using a dremel tool, carefully attach door to front of angel house with door hinge assemblies.

25. Using industrial-strength glue, attach door knob to front side of door.

26. Glue moon charm to front side of door using photograph on page 23 for placement.

27. Using wood glue, attach roof on angel house.

28. Alternating colors, glue clay patio bricks along bottom edge of roof lines using photograph for placement.

29. Seal angel house with matte acrylic spray.

MATERIALS FOR UPPER APARTMENT

Wood:
☐ Front, $5^1/2$" x $3^5/8$" x $1/4$"
☐ Back, $5^1/2$" x $3^5/8$" x $1/4$"
☐ Sides, $6^1/4$" x $6^3/4$" x $1/4$" (2)
☐ Base, $5^3/4$" x $1^3/4$" x $1/4$" (2) (*)
☐ Roof, $7^1/2$" x $4^3/4$" x $1/4$"
☐ Roof, $7^1/2$" x 5" x $1/4$"

Hardware, $1/24$ scale:
Door hinge assemblies (2)
Door knob

Decorative accessories:
Paper flowers

Paints & finishes:
Black, blue, dark green, light green, pink, white and yellow acrylic paints
Brass liquid leafing
Gesso
Matte acrylic spray

HOW-TO

1. Before beginning, carefully read General Instructions on pages 7-12.

2. Note: This angel house has been rotated so the front and back become the sides and the sides become the front and back.

3. Using a table saw, cut wood for front, back, sides, and roof using basic studio blueprints on page 114.

4. Cut wood for base using altered dimensions given.

5. Using graphite paper and a stylus, transfer windows on front and sides and door on front using window and door placement patterns on page 30. Transfer inverted "V's" on sides using notch placement pattern on page 30.

6. Using a drill and ¼" drill bit, drill pilot holes in each corner of windows.

7. Using a jigsaw, cut out windows and door. Save and set door aside. Cut out "V's" on sides.

8. Using wood glue, assemble front, back, and sides of angel house. Note: Do not glue roof on at this time.

9. Glue base pieces inside assembled angel house, aligning front, back, and sides with inside edges of base. Bottoms must be flush.

10. Using a paintbrush, paint angel house and base with gesso.

11. Paint both sides of angel house roof with gesso.

12. Using a paintbrush, paint angel house on the inside with yellow acrylic paint, then dry-brush with white acrylic paint.

13. Using a ruler and a pencil, mark horizontal and vertical placement lines on one side of angel house roof to form squares as desired.

14. Paint every other square with black acrylic paint.

15. Paint remaining squares with white.

16. Dry-brush over black and white squares with blue and light green acrylic paints.

17. Paint both sides of door, including all outside edges, with light green.

18. Using a lining brush, paint thin accent lines on both sides of door with dark green acrylic paint that has been thinned with water.

19. Paint thin accent lines on both sides of door with pink acrylic paint that has been thinned with water.

20. Using a sponge, sponge-paint both sides of door with dark green and pink that has been thinned with water.

21. Using a paintbrush, paint angel house with brass liquid leafing.

22. Paint bottom of base with brass liquid leafing.

23. Paint inside edges of each window and door with black acrylic paint.

24. Paint a ¼" border around each window and door with black.

25. Paint unpainted side of roof, including all outside edges, with black.

26. Using découpage glue, découpage paper flowers onto angel house according to manufacturer's directions.

27. Using a dremel tool, carefully attach door to front of angel house with door hinge assemblies.

28. Using industrial-strength glue, attach door knob to front side of door.

29. Using wood glue, attach roof on angel house.

30. Seal angel house with matte acrylic spray.

31. Using industrial-strength glue, stack angel houses and glue in place.

WINDOW AND DOOR PLACEMENT PATTERNS

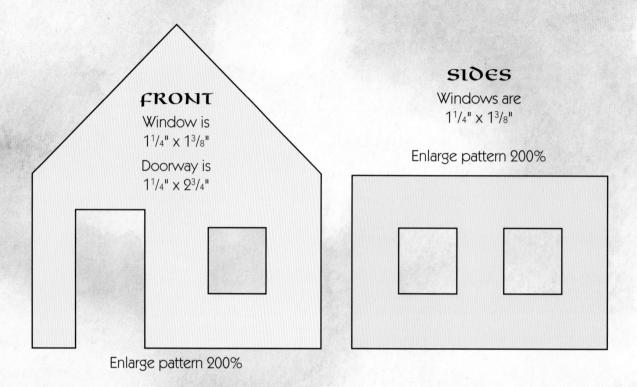

FRONT
Window is
$1^{1}/_{4}$" x $1^{3}/_{8}$"

Doorway is
$1^{1}/_{4}$" x $2^{3}/_{4}$"

Enlarge pattern 200%

SIDES
Windows are
$1^{1}/_{4}$" x $1^{3}/_{8}$"

Enlarge pattern 200%

NOTCH PLACEMENT PATTERN

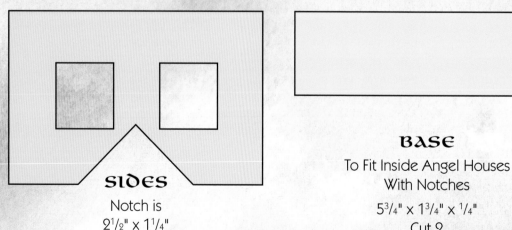

SIDES
Notch is
$2^{1}/_{2}$" x $1^{1}/_{4}$"

Cut pitch of roof
at a 45° angle.

Enlarge pattern 200%

BASE
To Fit Inside Angel Houses
With Notches

$5^{3}/_{4}$" x $1^{3}/_{4}$" x $1/_{4}$"
Cut 2

Once assembled, inside edges
of base must be beveled at
a 45° angle to fit pitch of roof.

Enlarge pattern 200%

CHERUB'S CHAMBERS

cherub's chambers

materials

Wood:
- ☐ Front, 6$\frac{1}{2}$" x 3$\frac{5}{8}$" x $\frac{1}{4}$" (*)
- ☐ Back, 6$\frac{1}{2}$" x 3$\frac{5}{8}$" x $\frac{1}{4}$" (*)
- ☐ Sides, 6$\frac{1}{2}$" x 6$\frac{3}{4}$" x $\frac{1}{4}$" (2) (*)
- ☐ Base, 12$\frac{1}{4}$" x 7" x $\frac{1}{4}$" (*)
- ☐ Roof, 7$\frac{1}{2}$" x 4$\frac{3}{4}$" x $\frac{1}{4}$"
- ☐ Roof, 7$\frac{1}{2}$" x 5" x $\frac{1}{4}$"
- ☐ Addition Front,
     5$\frac{1}{2}$" x 3$\frac{5}{8}$" x $\frac{1}{4}$"
- ☐ Addition Back,
     5$\frac{1}{2}$" x 3$\frac{5}{8}$" x $\frac{1}{4}$"
- ☐ Addition Side,
     6$\frac{1}{4}$" x 5$\frac{3}{8}$" x $\frac{1}{4}$"
- ☐ Addition Roof,
     8" x 4" x $\frac{1}{4}$" (2)

Hardware, $\frac{1}{24}$ scale:
Door hinge assemblies (4)

Decorative accessories:
Wooden chimney,
   1" x 1$\frac{1}{2}$" x 2$\frac{1}{4}$" high
White paper ribbon, 12 yards

Paints & finishes:
Light blue, medium blue,
   dark brown, cream, gray,
   medium green, light pink,
   medium pink, tan, white,
   and medium yellow
   acrylic paints
Extra-fine point permanent
   marker, black
Matte acrylic spray sealer

how-to

1. <u>Before beginning, carefully read General Instructions on pages 7-12.</u>

2. <u>Note: This angel house has been rotated so the front and back become the sides and the sides become the front and back.</u>

3. Using a table saw, cut wood for roof using basic studio blueprints on page 114.

4. Cut wood for front, back, sides, and base using altered dimensions given. Cut notch in base using pattern on page 35.

5. Cut wood for addition front, addition back, addition side, and addition roof using addition patterns on page 35. Cut notch in corresponding corners of addition front and addition back using pattern on page 34.

6. Using a miter saw, miter one long end of each addition roof piece at a 60° angle.

7. Bevel wooden chimney at a 45° angle to fit pitch of angel house roof.

8. Using graphite paper and a stylus, transfer doors on front of addition and back of angel house using door placement patterns on page 34.

9. Using a jigsaw, cut out doors. Save and set doors aside.

10. Using wood glue, assemble front, back, and sides of angel house and glue roof together. <u>Note: Do not glue roof on at this time.</u>

11. Assemble front, back, and side of addition and glue addition roof together. <u>Note: Do not glue addition roof on at this time.</u>

12. Using a paintbrush, paint angel house and addition on the inside, base, including all outside edges, both sides of angel house roof and addition roof, including all outside edges, and chimney with white acrylic paint.

13. Using paper scissors, decrease width of paper ribbon to $\frac{3}{4}$" by cutting appropriate amount off along top edge of paper ribbon.

14. Starting at bottom edges of roof lines and allowing scalloped edge to hang over edges of roof lines, measure and cut individual strips of paper ribbon to fit across roofs as shingles. Use white acrylic paint as glue by painting paper ribbon onto roof.

15. Measure and cut paper ribbon so scalloped edge of ribbon fits front and back edges of angel house roof lines and side edge of addition roof line for eaves.

16. Sponge-paint angel house and addition on the inside and the outside with light pink acrylic paint.

17. Cut a ¼" x ⅝" rectangle from sponge for a brick pattern. Dip sponge into white acrylic paint. Blot excess paint onto a paper towel. Referring to photographs on page 31 and below, sponge bricks onto fronts and backs of angel house and addition. Randomly sponge bricks onto sides of angel house and addition.

18. Cut a ¼" x ⅝" rectangle from sponge for a brick pattern. Dip sponge into white acrylic paint. Blot excess paint onto a paper towel. Referring to photographs on page 31 and below, sponge bricks onto fronts and backs of angel house and addition. Randomly sponge bricks onto sides of angel house and addition.

19. Dip sponge into medium pink acrylic paint. Blot excess paint onto a paper towel. Sponge bricks onto all sides of chimney.

20. Using a paintbrush, paint door frames and doors with light blue acrylic paint. Add wood grain on doors with medium blue acrylic paint.

21. Paint window frames on fronts of angel house, addition, and both doors with white acrylic paint. Paint window panes with cream acrylic paint. Paint shadows in window panes with gray acrylic paint. Paint shutters and awning on angel house with medium pink acrylic paint. Paint rattles with light blue, medium pink and white acrylic paints. Paint window handles with medium yellow acrylic paint. Paint pacifiers on doors for door knobs with medium yellow, medium pink, and white acrylic paints.

22. Randomly paint flowers around house and addition. Paint delphinium stocks with medium blue acrylic paint. Paint purple coneflowers with medium pink, tan, and dark brown acrylic paints. Paint daisies with white and medium yellow acrylic paints.

23. Randomly paint tiny butterflies in flowers with medium blue acrylic paint.

24. Randomly add tiny accent dots and draw butterfly bodies with extra-fine point permanent black marker.

25. Lightly sponge-paint around bricks and flowers with medium pink.

26. Outline windows, door frames, pacifiers, and rattles with extra-fine point permanent black marker.

27. Using graphite paper and a stylus, transfer saying below to front of angel house using photograph for placement.

28. Using a lining brush, paint saying with light blue acrylic paint.

29. Using a dremel tool, carefully attach doors to front of addition and back of angel house with door hinge assemblies.

30. Glue assembled angel house and addition together. Glue angel house on base, aligning front, back, and sides with outside edges of base.

31. Using wood glue, attach roofs on angel house.

32. Attach chimney to angel house roof using photograph for placement.

33. Seal angel house with matte acrylic spray.

DOOR PLACEMENT PATTERNS

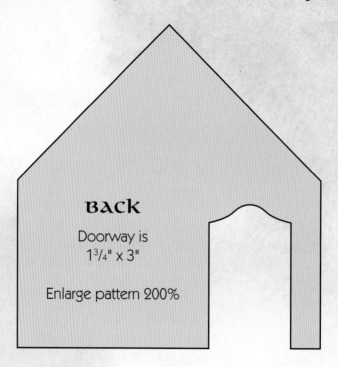

BACK

Doorway is
1³/₄" x 3"

Enlarge pattern 200%

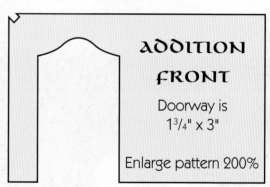

ADDITION FRONT

Doorway is
1³/₄" x 3"

Enlarge pattern 200%

A special blessing for you this day, Your own little Angel has come to stay.

Enlarge saying 125%

ADDITION PATTERNS

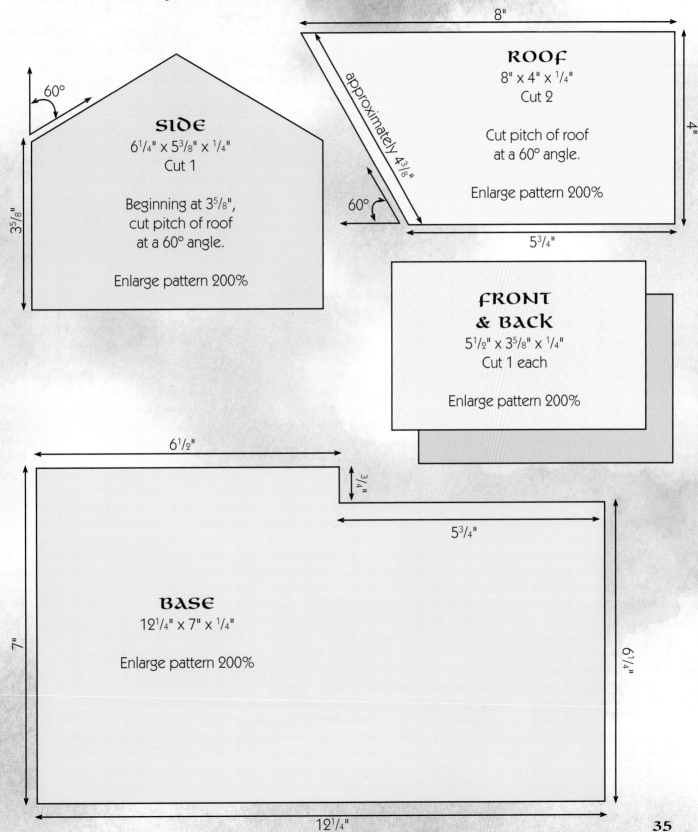

ROOF
8" x 4" x ¹/₄"
Cut 2

Cut pitch of roof
at a 60° angle.

Enlarge pattern 200%

8"

4"

approximately 4³/₈"

60°

5³/₄"

60°

SIDE
6¹/₄" x 5³/₈" x ¹/₄"
Cut 1

Beginning at 3⁵/₈",
cut pitch of roof
at a 60° angle.

Enlarge pattern 200%

3⁵/₈"

**FRONT
& BACK**
5¹/₂" x 3⁵/₈" x ¹/₄"
Cut 1 each

Enlarge pattern 200%

6¹/₂"

³/₄"

5³/₄"

BASE
12¹/₄" x 7" x ¹/₄"

Enlarge pattern 200%

7"

6¹/₄"

12¹/₄"

An Angel has come here from above
To sew our hearts together with love

sew much like home

materials

Wood:
☐ Front, 12" x 6" x ¹/₄"
☐ Back, 12" x 6" x ¹/₄"
☐ Sides, 5¹/₂" x 7¹/₂" x ¹/₄"
☐ Base, 8" x 13¹/₄" x ¹/₄" (*)
☐ Roof, 13¹/₄" x 4¹/₂" x ¹/₄" (*)
☐ Roof, 13¹/₄" x 5¹/₂" x ¹/₄" (*)

Balsa wood:
¹/₂" x ¹/₂" x 26"

Windows:
Small print fabric, ¹/₄ yard
Wooden dowel,
    ¹/₈"-diameter x 22" long

Hardware, ¹/₁₂ scale:
Door hinge assemblies (5)
Keyplate and door knob
Shutter handles, ¹/₂" (2)

Decorative accessories:
Red plaid fabric, ¹/₂ yard
Measuring tape print
    ribbon, 5/8"-wide x 1 yard
Cream grosgrain ribbon,
    3"-wide x 28"

Wooden spools, 1¹/₄" (12)
Assorted buttons, ¹/₂"-³/₈" (50)
Embroidery floss,
    assorted colors
Cream eyelet lace,
    6"-wide x 4 yards;
    ¹/₂"-wide x 1¹/₂ yards
Needle, 2" hand-sewing
Thimble

Embellishments, optional:
Needles, 3" darning (9)
Dark green cording,
    1/8"-wide x 1/3 yard
Silk ribbon roses, gold (7)
Dried leaves, small
    (approximately 25)

Paints & finishes:
Black, dark brown, cream,
    metallic copper, metallic
    gold, dark red, and bright
    yellow acrylic paints
Matte acrylic spray
Liquid copper
Decoupage matte finish

how-to

1. <u>Before beginning, carefully read General Instructions on pages 7-12.</u>

2. Using a table saw, cut wood for front, back, and sides using basic one-story blueprints on page 115.

3. Cut wood for base and roof using altered dimensions given.

4. Using a miter saw, miter one long end of each roof piece at a 57° angle.

5. Using graphite paper and a stylus, transfer windows on front and back and door on front using window and door placement patterns on page 40.

6. Using a drill and ¹/₄" drill bit, drill pilot holes at top of windows and on door window.

7. Using a jigsaw, cut out round windows, heart-shaped window and door. Save and set heart-shaped window and door aside.

8. Cut window opening in door using door pattern on page 40. Cut heart-shaped piece in half using shutter pattern on page 40.

37

9. Using wood glue, assemble front, back, and sides of angel house and glue roof together. <u>Note: Do not glue roof on at this time.</u>

10. Using a paintbrush, paint base, including all outside edges, inside of angel house, and bottom of roof with cream acrylic paint.

11. Using fabric scissors, measure and cut red plaid fabric into four pieces to fit all outside walls, making all fabric pieces 1/4" larger on all sides. Cut fabric out for front door and all windows, leaving 1/4" to turn in and attach to door and window frames. Clip curves.

12. Measure and cut brown fabric scrap to cover front and sides of shutters.

13. Using an old paintbrush and following manufacturer's instructions, decoupage red plaid fabric onto angel house. Decoupage brown fabric onto shutters. If necessary, cut small strips of fabric to fit inside door and window frames for a clean, finished appearance.

14. Cut grosgrain ribbon in half. Decoupage ribbons to bottom of roof, wrapping 1/2" over outside edges and up on top of roof.

15. Measure and cut 6"-wide eyelet lace into strips to layer and cover top of roof, leaving enough excess to wrap around and under eaves. Measure and cut 1/2"-wide eyelet lace into strips to fit under side eaves and across top front and back pitch of

roof, leaving enough excess to wrap around and under eaves. Decoupage laces to roof. Allow decoupage to dry thoroughly, then apply a second coat over entire roof.

16. Using a craft knife, cut wooden dowel into one 2", one 6", and two 4" lengths to make curtain rods.

17. Cut small print fabric into three 12"-wide x 5" and one 10"-wide x 3" rectangles to make curtains. Fold top edge of each curtain down 1". Sew 1/2" from top edge. Sew a second row of stitches 1/4" from top edge, forming a casing. Sew a basting stitch along bottom edge of each curtain. Gather small curtain onto 2" wooden dowel. Gather remaining curtains onto remaining wooden dowels. Using a hot glue gun and glue sticks, glue ends of each curtain onto rods to secure. Set curtain for door window aside. Glue rods over windows. Gather bottom edge of each curtain to evenly fit with top rod and glue in place.

18. Using wood glue, attach assembled angel house to base. Using a glue gun and glue sticks, attach buttons around front windows, overlapping as desired.

19. Mix gold and copper metallic paints together and

paint door. Using a lining brush and black acrylic paint, paint designs on door to resemble a thimble. Using a hot glue gun and glue sticks, attach curtain over door window.

20. Using a dremel tool, carefully attach door to front of angel house with door hinge assemblies. Attach hinge assemblies and shutter handles to shutters.

21. Using wood glue, attach roof on angel house.

22. Glue shutters to back of angel house.

23. Cut $1/2$"-thick balsa wood into four $6^1/2$"-long x $1/2$"-wide pieces for porch posts. Bevel tops of porch posts at a 57° angle to fit pitch of angel house roof.

24. Paint porch posts with bright yellow acrylic paint.

25. Measure and cut measuring tape ribbon into four lengths to fit and decoupage ribbon onto front of porch posts.

26. Glue one porch post in front of angel house, $3/4$" from each side and aligning with front edge of base. Glue remaining posts 3" from each end post.

27. Dilute black acrylic paint with water and wash paint onto wooden spools. Wrap spools with assorted embroidery floss colors.

28. Referring to photograph, glue four spools in-between posts and two spools at each end of porch.

29. Using graphite paper and a stylus, transfer saying below to roof of angel house using photograph for placement.

30. Using a lining brush, paint saying with dark red acrylic paint.

31. Paint thimble and darning needles with metallic copper and metallic gold paint mixture. Highlight thimble and darning needles with liquid copper. Glue 2" needle and thimble on roof using photograph for placement.

32. Using industrial-strength glue, adhere darning needles together in the shape of a trellis. Wind dark green cording around trellis to make a vine. Glue trellis to one side of angel house. Randomly glue silk ribbon roses and dried leaves to trellis as desired.

Enlarge saying 165%

An Angel has come here from above
To sew our hearts together with love

WINDOW AND DOOR PLACEMENT PATTERNS

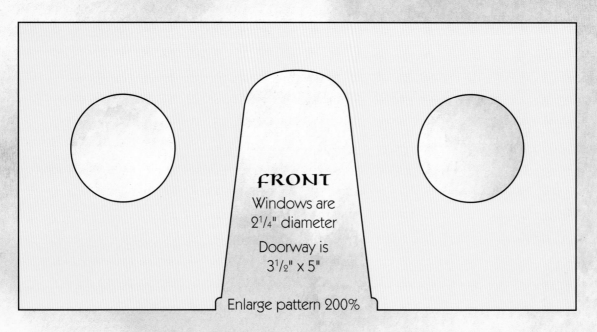

FRONT
Windows are
2¼" diameter

Doorway is
3½" x 5"

Enlarge pattern 200%

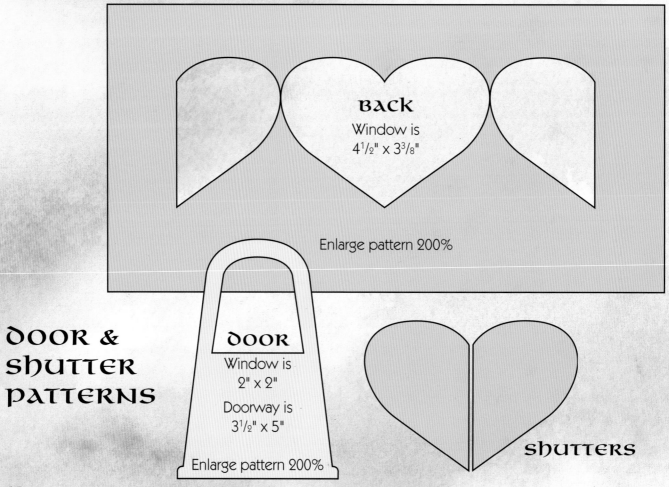

BACK
Window is
4½" x 3⅜"

Enlarge pattern 200%

DOOR & SHUTTER PATTERNS

DOOR
Window is
2" x 2"

Doorway is
3½" x 5"

Enlarge pattern 200%

SHUTTERS

SERENITY HOLLOW

Woodland creatures
near and far
Do you see the Angel's Star
Shining above her house so bright
Lighting the way
on Christmas night.

SERENITY HOLLOW

MATERIALS

Wood:
☐ Front, 12" x 6" x $^1/_4$"
☐ Back, 12" x 6" x $^1/_4$"
☐ Sides, 5$^1/_2$" x 7$^1/_2$" x $^1/_4$"
☐ Base, 12" x 24" x $^1/_2$" (*)
☐ Roof, 15 x 4$^1/_2$" x $^1/_4$" (2) (*)
☐ Chimney, 4$^1/_2$" x 8$^3/_4$" x 2"

Balsa wood:
$^3/_8$" x $^3/_8$" x 5"

Windows:
Flat toothpicks (8)
Woven Christmas fabric,
  $^1/_4$ yard
Thread, coordinating

Hardware, $^1/_{12}$ scale:
Door hinge assemblies (2)
Keyplate and door knob

Shingles & moulding:
Square-butt cedar shake
  shingles (approximately 300)
Pine molding, $^1/_2$"-round,
  12$^1/_4$" (12), 6" (16);
  $^1/_4$"-round, 6" (4)
Sanded tile grout

Decorative accessories:
Chain
Soft blanket fabric, $^1/_4$ yard
Flat rocks, variety of sizes
Artificial trees with pinecones
Artificial snow
Cup hooks (4)
Miniature wreaths (4)
Miniature light set,
  battery-packed (3)

Floral wire, 18-gauge 18";
  very fine, 12"
Birch bark

Paints & finishes:
Dark gray, dark green, light tan,
  and medium tan
  acrylic paints
Light brown wood stain
Clear acrylic spray
Matte acrylic spray
Clear varnish
Matte varnish

HOW-TO

1. <u>Before beginning, carefully read General Instructions on pages 7-12.</u>

2. Using a table saw, cut wood for front, back, sides, and roof using basic one-story blueprints on page 115.

3. Cut wood for base using altered dimensions given.

4. Cut wood for chimney using the double chimney pattern on page 123.

5. Hold chimney in position on back of angel house and trace around it. Using wood glue, attach $^1/_2$"-round moldings to front, sides, and back of angel house, leaving the marked area for chimney plus $^1/_4$" without molding.

6. Using graphite paper and a stylus, transfer windows on front and sides and door on front using window and door placement patterns on page 45.

7. Using a drill and $^1/_4$" drill bit, drill pilot holes in each corner of windows.

8. Using a jigsaw, cut out windows and door. Save and set door aside.

9. Cut a 3"-wide x $^3/_4$" high notch centered along back edge of roof to accommodate chimney using notch placement pattern on page 45. Notch must be cut at a 45° angle.

10. Using a miter saw, miter top of each side wall at a 57° angle.

11. Using a hammer, hit chain against outside of angel house to indent and distress the wood.

12. Stain angel house on the inside and outside and base with light brown wood stain according to manufacturer's directions.

13. Glue flat toothpicks into crossbars, then glue crossbars into windows.

14. Using a paintbrush, paint crossbars, inside window edges, and door with dark green acrylic paint.

15. Using wood glue, assemble front, back, and sides of angel house and glue roof together. Note: Do not glue roof on at this time.

16. Glue ¼"-round moldings on outside corners of angel house.

17. Spray inside and outside of angel house and door with clear acrylic spray.

18. Using fabric scissors, cut soft blanket fabric into a 12¼" x 6" piece. Glue fabric to bottom of angel house for carpeting.

19. Cut woven Christmas fabric into four 6" x 4½" pieces. Using a needle and coordinating thread, gather-stitch along one 6" side of each fabric piece to make curtains.

20. Using industrial-strength glue, attach curtains to windows on inside of angel house.

21. Using a dremel tool, carefully attach door to front of angel house with door hinge assemblies.

22. Using industrial-strength glue, attach keyplate and door knob to front side of door.

23. Glue chimney into position in back of angel house.

24. Using a hammer, break rocks to desired size. Randomly glue rocks to chimney, leaving a small space in between rocks for grout.

25. Mix sanded tile grout according to manufacturer's directions. Smear grout around side and top edges of chimney and over rocks, pushing grout in between rocks. Wipe grout from top of rocks with a sponge and allow grout to dry thoroughly.

26. Paint top of chimney with dark gray acrylic paint.

27. Paint over rocks with clear varnish.

28. Paint over grout with matte varnish.

29. Starting at bottom edges of roof and working across, glue shingles to angel house roof. Glue balsa wood to ends of roof, mitering pitched ends with a craft knife.

30. Paint shingles, outside edges, and bottom of roof with dark green acrylic paint.

31. Using wood glue, attach roof on angel house.

32. Attach assembled angel house to base.

33. Randomly stack rocks onto base as desired and glue in place to secure.

34. Glue artificial trees with pinecones onto base as desired.

35. With a swirling motion, paint and blend walkway and sides of base with dark gray, light tan and medium tan acrylic paints.

36. Using spray adhesive, Lightly spray base, roof, and trees, in small areas at a time, with spray adhesive. Cover sprayed areas with artificial snow. From a slight distance, spray artificial snow with matte acrylic spray.

37. Center and screw cup hooks over top of each window. Place miniature wreaths onto hooks.

38. Wire a miniature light set into the wreaths and hide battery-pack behind angel house or inside angel house.

39. Bend and shape 18-gauge floral wire into a star. Wrap remaining miniature lights around star and attach with very fine wire.

40. Staple star onto center of roof pitch.

41. Using graphite paper and a stylus, transfer saying to birch bark using photograph for placement.

42. Using a lining brush, paint saying with dark green acrylic paint.

Woodland creatures
near and far
Do you see the Angel's Star?
Shining above her house so bright
Lighting the way
on Christmas night.

Saying actual size

WINDOW AND DOOR PLACEMENT PATTERNS

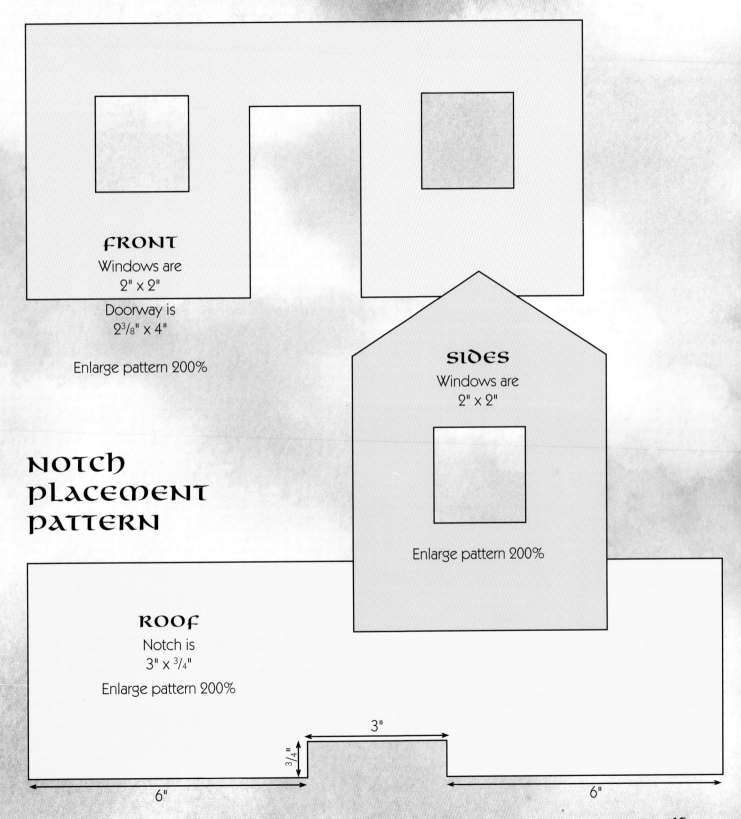

FRONT
Windows are
2" x 2"

Doorway is
$2^3/_8$" x 4"

Enlarge pattern 200%

SIDES
Windows are
2" x 2"

Enlarge pattern 200%

NOTCH PLACEMENT PATTERN

ROOF
Notch is
3" x $^3/_4$"

Enlarge pattern 200%

3"

$^3/_4$"

6"

6"

COMFORT INN

MATERIALS

Wood:
- ☐ Front, 8" x 7" x ¹/₂"
- ☐ Back, 8" x 7" x ¹/₂"
- ☐ Sides, 9" x 13³/₄" x ¹/₂" (2)
- ☐ Base, 9" x 9" x ¹/₂"
- ☐ Roof, 12" x 9" x ¹/₄" (2)

Balsa wood:
¹/₂" x 2" x 4"

Hardware, ¹/₁₂ scale:
Door hinge assemblies (2)
Door knob

Decorative accessories:
Wooden chimneys,
   1¹⁵/₁₆" square x
   4¹/₁₆" high (2)

Paints & finishes:
Beige, brown, light salmon,
   mint, salmon, and
   white acrylic paints
Matte acrylic spray

HOW-TO

1. <u>Before beginning, carefully read General Instructions on pages 7-12.</u>

2. Using a table saw, cut wood for front, back, sides, base, and roof using basic house blueprints on page 116.

3. Using a miter saw, miter one long end of each roof piece at a 34° angle.

4. Bevel wooden chimneys at a 34° angle to fit pitch of angel house roof.

5. Using graphite paper and a stylus, transfer door on front using door placement pattern on page 48.

6. Using a jigsaw, cut out door.

7. Using a craft knife, cut ¹/₂"-thick balsa wood piece into a door using door pattern on page 48. Cut window openings in door.

8. Using wood glue, assemble front, back, and sides of angel house and glue roof together. <u>Note: Do not glue roof on at this time.</u>

47

9. Glue assembled angel house on base, aligning front, back, and sides with outside edges of base.

10. Using a paintbrush, paint angel house on the inside and the outside, the base, including all outside edges, and both wooden chimneys with beige acrylic paint.

11. Paint both sides of roof, including all outside edges, with salmon acrylic paint.

12. Paint both sides of door, including all outside edges, with mint acrylic paint.

13. Paint four vertical windows, including all cross members, on front and on back of angel house and six vertical windows, including all cross members, evenly spaced on each side of angel house with brown acrylic paint using photograph on page 46 for placement of windows on front. Make certain tops of all windows are aligned and all second-floor windows are centered above first-floor windows.

14. Paint windowpanes in each window with white acrylic paint.

15. Paint curtains in each window with light salmon acrylic paint.

16. Paint one heart above door using photograph for placement and one heart on each side with salmon. Position hearts on sides for attic window placement.

17. Float-shade around windows and hearts and paint 1/4" corner moulding on each corner of angel house with brown.

18. Paint tops of and bricks around wooden chimneys with brown alternating position of bricks on each row using photograph for placement.

19. Using a ruler and a pencil, mark horizontal and vertical placement lines on top of roof.

door placement pattern

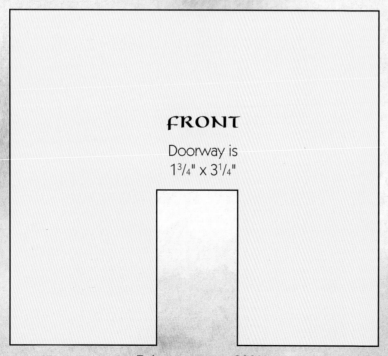

FRONT

Doorway is
1³/₄" x 3¹/₄"

Enlarge pattern 200%

door pattern

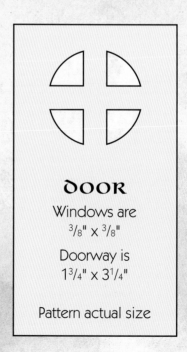

DOOR

Windows are
³/₈" x ³/₈"

Doorway is
1³/₄" x 3¹/₄"

Pattern actual size

Allow 1" between each placement line to form 1" squares. Mark horizontal placement lines around outside perimeter of angel house. Allow ³/₄" between each placement line.

20. Paint every other square on roof with mint so they alternate between salmon and mint.

21. Float-shade along bottom edge of each row of squares on roof and along placement lines around angel house with brown for siding.

22. Using a dremel tool, carefully attach door to front of angel house with door hinge assemblies.

23. Using industrial-strength glue, attach door knob to front side of door.

24. Using wood glue, attach roof on angel house.

25. Glue wooden chimneys on roof in back of angel house using photograph for placement.

26. Using graphite paper and a stylus, transfer saying below to angel house using photograph for placement.

27. Using a lining brush, paint saying with mint acrylic paint.

28. Seal angel house with matte acrylic spray.

Starlight, Starbright, I wish, I may, I wish I might... Find an Angel here tonight!

Enlarge saying 110%

HEAVENLY GUIDE for Beginner Angels

THE GOLDEN CALVES

QUIET: AN ANGEL'S READING ROOM

MATERIALS

Wood:
☐ Front, 8" x 7" x ¹/₂"
☐ Back, 8" x 7" x ¹/₂"
☐ Sides, 9" x 13³/₄" x ¹/₂" (2)
☐ Base, 11¹/₂" x 11¹/₂" x ¹/₄" (*)
☐ Roof, 12" x 9" x ¹/₄" (2)
☐ Chimney, 2¹/₂" x 13¹/₂" x 1"

Hardware, ¹/₁₂ scale:
Door hinge assemblies (4)
Door knobs (2)

Shingles:
Octagon butt shingles,
  ³/₄" x 1¹/₄"
  (approximately 500)

Decorative accessories:
Used book, approximately
  9¹/₂" x 12" x ³/₄"
Wooden books (open),
  1¹/₂" x 1¹/₂" (8)
Wooden books,
  1¹/₂" x 2" (2)
Wooden books,
  1" x 1" (10)
Smooth rocks,
  ¹/₂" to 1¹/₂" long (50-60)
Sanded tile grout, tan

Embellishments, optional:
Flower pots, painted
Clay flowers, painted

Paints & finishes:
Burgundy, cream, dark green,
  dark rust, gold, medium
  blue, mustard, and
  rust acrylic paints
Matte acrylic spray

HOW-TO

1. Before beginning, care-fully read General Instructions on pages 7-12.

2. Using a table saw, cut wood for front, back, sides, and roof using basic house blueprints on page 116.

3. Cut wood for base using altered dimensions given.

4. Cut wood for chimney using the two-story chimney pattern on page 123.

5. Using a miter saw, miter one long end of each roof piece at a 34° angle.

6. Cut chimney into two pieces at a 34° angle to fit pitch of roof as shown on pattern.

7. Using graphite paper and a stylus, transfer windows and doors on front and back using window and door placement patterns on pages 7-12.

8. Using a drill and ¹/₄" drill bit, drill pilot holes in each corner of windows.

9. Using a jigsaw, cut out windows and doors. Save and set doors aside.

10. Using wood glue, assemble front, back, and sides of angel house and glue roof together. Note: Do not glue roof on at this time.

11. Glue assembled angel house on base, allowing 2" in front, 1/2" in back, 2" on left side, and 1/2" on right side of base.

12. Using a ruler and a pencil, mark horizontal placement lines around outside perimeter of angel house. Allow approximately 3/4" between each placement line.

13. Starting at bottom edges of angel house and working across, glue shingles for siding to front, back, and sides. Shingles on sides of angel house should end where roof pitch begins and should not be placed where chimney is to be positioned.

14. Using a craft knife, trim shingles around window and door openings.

15. Using a paintbrush, paint siding, upper portions of sides that have been left unshingled, and angel house on the inside with rust acrylic paint.

16. Paint both sides of roof, including all outside edges, with cream acrylic paint.

17. Paint both sides of doors and base and covers and spines of used book, all open wooden books, both 1 1/2" x 2" wooden books, and two 1" x 1" wooden books with dark green acrylic paint.

18. Paint covers and spines of two 1" x 1" wooden books with burgundy acrylic paint, two with dark rust acrylic paint, two with medium blue acrylic paint, and two with mustard acrylic paint.

19. Paint pages on all wooden books and all outside edges of doors and base with cream.

20. Using a lining brush, paint "lines of writing" on pages of open wooden books with rust.

21. Paint two stripes on spines of dark rust colored and mustard colored books and one stripe across both doors with gold acrylic paint using photograph on page 50 for placement.

22. Using a dremel tool, carefully attach doors to front and back of angel house with door hinge assemblies.

23. Using industrial-strength glue, attach door knobs to front sides of doors.

24. Using wood glue, attach roof on angel house.

25. Glue open wooden books to top of windows for awnings using photograph for placement.

26. Stack 1" x 1" wooden books on each side of front door (burgundy, dark green, mustard, medium blue, and dark rust) and glue in place. Books should be stacked unevenly using photograph for placement.

27. Place 1¹/₂" x 2" wooden books on top of stacked books and angle above front door. Glue in place using photograph for placement.

28. If desired, flower pots filled with clay flowers can be glued inside angel house windows.

29. Using graphite paper and a stylus, transfer sayings on page 54 to cover and spine of used book using photograph for placement.

30. Using a lining brush, paint sayings with gold acrylic paint.

31. Open used book to center and place it over pitch of roof. Using craft glue, attach center pages of book to roof.

32. Seal angel house with matte acrylic spray.

WINDOW AND DOOR PLACEMENT PATTERNS

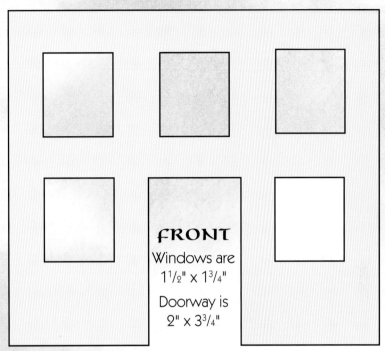

FRONT
Windows are
1¹/₂" x 1³/₄"
Doorway is
2" x 3³/₄"

Enlarge pattern 200%

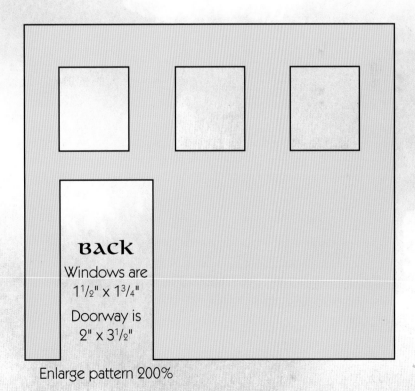

BACK
Windows are
1¹/₂" x 1³/₄"
Doorway is
2" x 3¹/₂"

Enlarge pattern 200%

33. Using industrial-strength glue, attach bottom portion of chimney to side of angel house, covering shingles, and top portion of chimney on top of used book.

34. Using craft glue, randomly place and adhere smooth rocks to chimney and to small section on used book using photograph for placement.

35. Using a hot glue gun and glue sticks, make a bead of hot glue around each rock to

secure the rock in place while craft glue dries.

36. Mix sanded tile grout according to manufacturer's directions.

37. Mask area around chimney with plastic wrap and masking tape.

38. Apply sanded tile grout around rocks, removing excess tile grout.

39. Remove plastic wrap and masking tape.

HEAVENLY

Enlarge sayings 135%

GUIDE

for

Beginner

Angels

By GABRIEL TRUMPETT

Sterling~Chapelle

a house of higher learning

a house of higher Learning

materials

Wood:
- ☐ Front, 8" x 7" x ¹⁄₂"
- ☐ Back, 8" x 7" x ¹⁄₂"
- ☐ Sides, 9" x 13³⁄₄" x ¹⁄₂" (2)
- ☐ Base, 9" x 12" x ¹⁄₂" (*)
- ☐ Roof, 12" x 9" x ¹⁄₄" (2)
- ☐ Bell tower walls
      (front and back),
      3" x 6" x ¹⁄₄" (2)
- ☐ Bell tower walls (side),
      2³⁄₄" x 4" x ¹⁄₄" (2)
- ☐ Bell tower roof,
      4" x 3¹⁄₂" x ¹⁄₄" (2)

Balsa wood:
¹⁄₂" x ¹⁄₂" x 9¹⁄₂" (2)

Windows & door, ¹⁄₁₂ scale:
8-light windows, 5¹⁄₁₆" x 2⁹⁄₁₆" (2)
5-panel door and frame, 3" x 7"

Hardware, ¹⁄₁₂ scale:
Keyplate and door knob
Skeleton keys on ring
Nail, tiny

Siding & shingles:
Clapboard siding, ¹⁄₂"
   (12 sheets)
Square butt shingles,
   ³⁄₄" x 1¹⁄₄"
   (approximately 500)

Decorative accessories:
Wooden banner,
   4" x 2¹⁄₂"
Chalkboard,
   7" x 5"
Brass bell, 1¹⁄₄"
Linen jute

Embellishments, optional:
Wooden apple, painted
Wooden books, painted

Paints & finishes:
Black, brown, and
   off-white acrylic paints
Black, brick red, and
   cream milk paints
Antiquing medium
Milk paint varnish
Matte acrylic spray

how-to

1. <u>Before beginning, carefully read General Instructions on pages 7-12.</u>

Within these walls an Angel sings of ABC's and learning new things.

Saying actual size

2. Note: This angel house has been rotated so the front and back become the sides and the sides become the front and back.

3. Using a table saw, cut wood for front, back, sides, and roof using basic house blueprints on page 116.

4. Cut wood for base using altered dimensions given.

5. Cut wood for bell tower front, back, and side walls and bell tower roof using bell tower patterns on page 120.

6. Using a miter saw, miter one long end of each roof piece at a 34° angle, including roof pieces for bell tower.

7. Using wood glue, attach clapboard siding to front, back, and sides. Allow a 1/2" overlap on each end of both sides to cover width of wood on pitched ends once front, back, and sides have been assembled. Attach clapboard siding to bell tower walls. Allow a 1/4" overlap on each end of both side walls to cover width of wood on pitched ends once front, back, and side walls have been assembled.

8. Using graphite paper and a stylus, transfer windows on sides and door on front using window and door placement patterns on page 58. Transfer

openings and inverted "V's" on bell tower walls using bell tower patterns on page 120.

9. Using a drill and 1/4" drill bit, drill pilot holes in each corner of windows and openings on bell tower walls.

10. Using a jigsaw, cut out windows and door. Cut out openings and "V's" on bell tower walls.

11. Using wood glue, assemble front, back, and sides of angel house and glue roof together. Note: Do not glue roof on at this time.

12. Assemble walls of bell tower and glue bell tower roof together. Note: Do not glue roof on at this time.

13. Glue assembled angel house on base, aligning back and sides with outside edges of base.

14. Using a paintbrush, paint clapboard siding on angel house and bell tower with brick red milk paint.

15. Paint angel house on the inside, both sides of door, including all outside edges, door frame, window frames, and base, including all outside edges, and balsa wood pieces for porch posts with cream milk paint.

16. Paint both sides of angel house roof and bell tower roof, including all outside edges, with black milk paint.

17. Paint wooden banner with off-white acrylic paint, then float-shade edges with brown acrylic paint.

18. Paint a few addition and/or subtraction problems and three or four spelling words on chalkboard with off-white.

19. Apply antiquing medium to all painted pieces according to manufacturer's directions.

20. Using wood glue, carefully attach door frame to front of angel house.

21. Using industrial-strength glue, attach keyplate and door knob to front side of door.

22. Glue chalkboard to back wall on inside of angel house.

23. Using a toothpick, apply wood glue around window frames and set them in place.

24. Using wood glue, attach roof on angel house. Attach roof on bell tower.

25. Bevel bottom of bell tower walls on both sides at a 34° angle to fit pitch of angel house roof, and glue bell tower on angel house using photograph on page 55 for placement.

26. Using a ruler and a pencil, mark horizontal placement lines on angel house roof and bell tower roof. Allow approximately $5/8$" between each placement line.

27. Starting at bottom edges of roof lines and working across, glue shingles to angel house roof and bell tower roof.

28. Using a paintbrush, paint shingles with black milk paint.

29. Using a craft knife, cut top of each porch post at a 34° angle to fit between roof and base and glue in place using photograph for placement.

30. Using a paintbrush, seal angel house and bell tower with milk paint varnish.

31. Using graphite paper and a stylus, transfer saying on page 57 to wooden banner.

32. Using a lining brush, paint saying with black acrylic paint.

33. Seal wooden banner with matte acrylic spray.

34. Using wood glue, attach wooden banner above door.

35. Using a dremel tool, carefully attach nail to door frame and hang ring of skeleton keys on nail.

36. Thread linen jute through hole in top of brass bell and tie, leaving a tail hanging.

37. Using industrial-strength glue, attach linen jute inside bell tower at center so bell hangs appropriately.

38. If desired, a wooden apple and some wooden books can be glued near the school house door.

WINDOW AND DOOR PLACEMENT PATTERNS

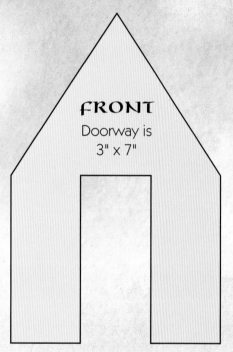

FRONT
Doorway is
3" x 7"

Enlarge pattern 400%

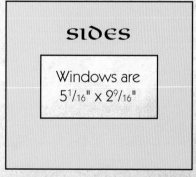

SIDES
Windows are
$5^{1}/_{16}$" x $2^{9}/_{16}$"

Enlarge pattern 400%

CHRISTMAS COTTAGE

CHRISTMAS COTTAGE

MATERIALS

Wood:
- ☐ Front, $9^3/4$" x $5^1/4$" x $1/2$"
- ☐ Back, $9^3/4$" x $5^1/4$" x $1/2$"
- ☐ Sides, $4^1/4$" x $7^3/8$" x $1/2$" (2)
- ☐ Base, 9" x $12^3/4$" x $1/2$" (*)
- ☐ Roof, $11^3/4$" x $3^1/4$" x $1/2$"
- ☐ Roof, $11^3/4$" x $3^3/4$" x $1/2$"
- ☐ Entry way front,
     $2^3/4$" x $4^1/8$" x $1/2$" (*)
- ☐ Entry way sides,
     2" x $2^3/4$" x $1/2$" (2) (*)
- ☐ Entry way roof,
     $2^3/4$" x $2^1/2$" x $1/2$"
- ☐ Entry way roof,
     $2^3/4$" x 3" x $1/2$"

Balsa wood:
$1/4$" x 2" x 6"

Windows:
Off-white lace,
   3"-wide x $2/3$ yard

Hardware, $1/24$ scale:
Door hinge assemblies (4)
Keyplates and
   door knobs (2)

Decorative accessories:
French horn charm, $1^1/2$"
Resin Christmas tree, $2^3/4$"
Christmas bulb garland, tiny
Lamp post, painted
Christmas wreath

Paints & finishes:
Antique gold, forest green,
   iron oxide, ivory, and
      metallic gold acrylic paints
Matte acrylic spray

HOW-TO

1. <u>Before beginning, carefully read General Instructions on pages 7-12.</u>

2. Using a table saw, cut wood for front, back, sides, and roof using basic cottage blueprints on page 117.

3. Cut wood for base using altered dimensions given.

4. Cut wood for entry way roof using entry way patterns on page 124.

5. Cut wood for entry way front and sides using altered dimensions given. Beginning at $2^3/4$", cut pitch of roof at a 45° angle.

6. Using graphite paper and a stylus, transfer windows and doors on front, back, one side, and entry way front using window and door placement patterns on pages 62-63.

7. Using a drill and $1/4$" drill bit, drill pilot holes in each corner of windows. <u>Note: All windows are arched at top.</u>

8. Using a jigsaw, cut out windows and doors.

9. Using a craft knife, cut $1/4$"-thick balsa wood piece into doors using window and door placement patterns.

10. Using wood glue, assemble front, back, and sides of angel house and glue roof together. <u>Note: Do not glue roof on at this time.</u>

11. Assemble front and sides of entry way and glue entry way roof together. <u>Note: Do not glue roof on at this time.</u>

An Angel has come here to stay,
and watch over us on Christmas Day.

Enlarge pattern 110%

12. Glue assembled angel house on base, allowing 3³/₄" in front and 1" in back and on each side of base.

13. Glue assembled entry way to front of angel house and on base using photograph on page 59 for placement.

14. Using a paintbrush, paint angel house and entry way on the inside and the outside with ivory acrylic paint.

15. Paint base, including all outside edges, with antique gold acrylic paint, then stipple top of base with ivory.

16. Paint both sides of angel house roof and entry way roof, including all outside edges, both sides of doors, including all outside edges, and all outside edges around base with forest green acrylic paint.

17. Paint bricks at each corner of angel house with iron oxide acrylic paint, leaving ¹/₁₆" to ¹/₈" space between each brick. Alternate position of bricks using photograph for placement.

18. Paint three horizontal bricks below each window with iron oxide, leaving ¹/₁₆" to ¹/₈" space between each brick.

19. Paint five vertical bricks arched above each window and each door with iron oxide, leaving ¹/₁₆" to ¹/₈" space between each brick. Make center brick slightly larger than others.

20. Paint bricks from front door angling outward toward right corner of base with iron oxide, alternating position of bricks in each row.

21. Using a pencil, draw a circle at least ¹/₂" larger in diameter than base of lamp post. Paint bricks with iron oxide, keeping outer end of each brick even with pencil line.

61

22. Paint around each brick on the path and in the circle with ivory for mortar.

23. Using a ruler and a pencil, mark three horizontal placement lines on angel house roof and two horizontal placement lines on entry way roof. Allow approximately 1" between each placement line.

24. Starting at bottom edges of roof lines and working across, float-shade scallops with ivory. Alternate position of scallops on each row using photograph for placement.

25. Using a dremel tool, carefully attach doors to front and back of angel house with door hinge assemblies.

26. Using industrial-strength glue, attach keyplates and door knobs to front sides of doors.

27. Using fabric scissors, cut lace into five 4" pieces.

28. Using industrial-strength glue, attach lace to windows on inside of angel house to make curtains.

29. Using wood glue, attach roof on angel house. Attach roof on entry way.

30. Using graphite paper and a stylus, transfer saying on page 61 to angel house roof using photograph for placement.

31. Using a lining brush, paint saying with metallic gold acrylic paint.

32. Seal angel house with matte acrylic spray.

33. Using industrial-strength glue, attach French horn charm to front door.

34. Glue resin Christmas tree to right corner of angel house.

35. Using craft scissors, cut Christmas bulb garland to fit across roof lines and glue in place.

36. Glue lamp post on base, centering in painted brick pattern.

37. Glue Christmas wreath to lamp post.

WINDOW AND DOOR PLACEMENT PATTERNS

FRONT
Windows are
1¹/₂" x 2¹/₂"

Enlarge pattern 200%

WINDOW AND DOOR PLACEMENT PATTERNS (CONTINUED)

BACK

Windows are
$1^1/_8$" x $1^7/_8$"

Doorway is
$1^1/_2$" x 3"

Enlarge pattern 200%

SIDE

One Side Only

Window is
$1^1/_8$" x $1^7/_8$"

Enlarge pattern 200%

ENTRY WAY FRONT

Doorway is
$1^1/_2$" x $2^3/_4$"

Pattern actual size

An Angel watches over you

All day long and all night too,

a heavenly haven

materials

Wood:
- ☐ Front, 9³/₄" x 5¹/₄" x ¹/₂"
- ☐ Back, 9³/₄" x 5¹/₄" x ¹/₂"
- ☐ Sides, 4¹/₄" x 7³/₈" x ¹/₂" (2)
- ☐ Base, 6¹/₄" x 13¹/₄" x ¹/₄" (*)
- ☐ Roof, 12³/₄" x 3¹/₂" x ¹/₂" (*)
- ☐ Roof, 12³/₄" x 4" x ¹/₂" (*)
- ☐ Two-story entry front,
     3¹/₄" x 7⁷/₈" x ¹/₂"
- ☐ Two-story entry roof,
     2¹/₂" x 3¹/₈" x ¹/₄"
- ☐ Two-story entry roof,
     2³/₄" x 3³/₈" x ¹/₄"
- ☐ Chimney, 2¹/₄" x 8³/₄" x 2"

Balsa wood:
¹/₈" x 3" x 6"

Hardware, ¹/₂₄ scale:
Door hinge assemblies (2)
Keyplate and door knob

Decorative accessories:
Dried flowers, tiny
Dried greenery, tiny

Paints & finishes:
Burnt sienna, burnt umber,
  cream, green, maroon,
  slate blue, and
  white acrylic paints
Matte acrylic spray

how-to

1. Before beginning, carefully read General Instructions on pages 7-12.

2. Using a table saw, cut wood for front, back, and sides using basic cottage blueprints on page 117.

3. Cut wood for base and roof using altered dimensions given.

4. Cut wood for two-story entry front and roof using two-story entry patterns on page 126.

5. Cut wood for chimney using the cottage chimney pattern on page 122.

6. Using graphite paper and a stylus, transfer door on front of angel house and on front of two-story entry using door placement pattern on page 68.

7. Using a jigsaw, cut out doors. Save and set one door aside.

8. Cut a 3¹/₄"-wide x 1" high notch centered along 12³/₄" edge of 4" roof to accommodate two-story entry using notch placement patterns on page 68.

9. Cut a 1$\frac{1}{2}$"-wide x 1" high notch along 3$\frac{1}{2}$" edge of 3$\frac{1}{2}$" roof to accommodate chimney using notch placement patterns on page 68. Notch must be cut at a 45° angle.

10. Using a craft knife, cut $\frac{1}{8}$"-thick balsa wood into one 1$\frac{3}{4}$"-wide x $\frac{1}{2}$"-high piece, angling each end, for window box on two-story entry. Cut two 2$\frac{1}{2}$"-wide x $\frac{3}{4}$"-high pieces, angling each end, for window boxes on front of angel house.

11. Cut $\frac{1}{8}$"-thick balsa wood into twelve $\frac{1}{4}$"-wide x 2"-high pieces for shutter bars.

12. Using wood glue, assemble front, back, and sides of angel house and glue roof together. Note: Do not glue roof on at this time.

13. Glue assembled angel house on base, allowing 1" in front and in back, 1$\frac{1}{2}$" on left side (to accommodate chimney), and 1" on right side of base.

14. Glue two-story entry to front of angel house and on base using door placement pattern on page 68 for position and glue two-story entry roof together. Note: Do not glue roof on at this time, but bevel it at a 45° angle to fit pitch of angel house roof.

15. Using a paintbrush, paint angel house on the inside and the outside, two-story entry, underside of two-story entry roof, including all outside edges, and chimney with cream acrylic paint.

16. Paint base, including all outside edges, with white acrylic paint, then stipple with green acrylic paint.

17. Paint both sides of angel house roof, including all outside edges, top side of two-story entry roof, and both sides of doors, including all outside edges, with burnt sienna acrylic paint.

18. Paint all window boxes with slate blue acrylic paint.

19. Paint all shutter bars with burnt umber acrylic paint.

Enlarge saying 115%

20. Paint one arched window on front of door and one arched window on front of two-story entry above door with white. Position windows using photograph on page 64 for placement.

21. Paint one arched window on each side of two-story entry and two arched windows on back of angel house with burnt sienna.

22. Paint curtains tied back in window on door and in window above door with maroon acrylic paint.

23. Float-shade windows around curtains with slate blue.

24. Paint shutters on windows on each side of two-story entry and on windows on back of angel house with burnt sienna.

25. Paint a $^1/_8$" line around outside of each window with burnt sienna and, using this line as a guide, float-shade around each window with burnt sienna.

26. Paint two thin vertical lines down each shuttered window and one thin horizontal line across door just below window with burnt umber using photograph for placement.

27. Paint wood grain on each shutter and on both sides of door with burnt umber.

28. Using a ruler and a pencil, mark horizontal placement lines on angel house roof and two-story entry roof. Allow approximately $^3/_4$" between each placement line.

29. Starting at bottom edges of roof lines and working across, float-shade shingles with burnt umber, leaving $^1/_8$" space between each shingle. Alternate position of shingles on each row using photograph for placement.

30. Paint rocks on chimney with slate blue that has been watered down. To add depth, add more color to lower portion of each rock.

31. Using a dremel tool, carefully attach door to front of two-story entry with door hinge assemblies.

32. Using industrial-strength glue, attach keyplate and door knob to front side of door.

33. Using wood glue, attach roof on angel house. Attach beveled roof on two-story entry.

34. Glue chimney on left side of angel house.

35. Glue $1^3/_4$"-wide window box below window in upper portion of two-story entry.

36. Glue $2^1/_2$"-wide window boxes below windows on front of angel house, aligning bottoms with base.

37. Glue three shutter bars on each window on front and on back of angel house using photograph for placement.

38. Using graphite paper and a stylus, transfer saying on page 66 to angel house using photograph for placement.

39. Using a lining brush, paint saying with green acrylic paint.

40. Randomly paint small leaves and vines around saying for a climbing vine appearance.

41. Seal angel house with matte acrylic spray.

42. Using craft glue, fill window boxes with dried flowers and greenery.

DOOR PLACEMENT PATTERN

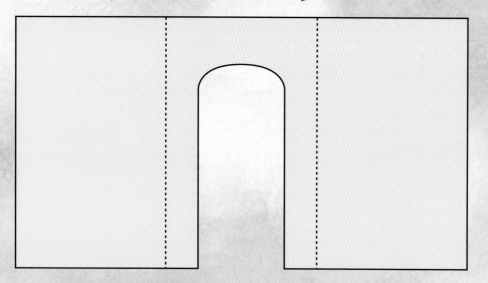

FRONT

Doorway is
$1^7/_8$" x $4^1/_4$"

Enlarge pattern 200%

NOTCH PLACEMENT PATTERNS

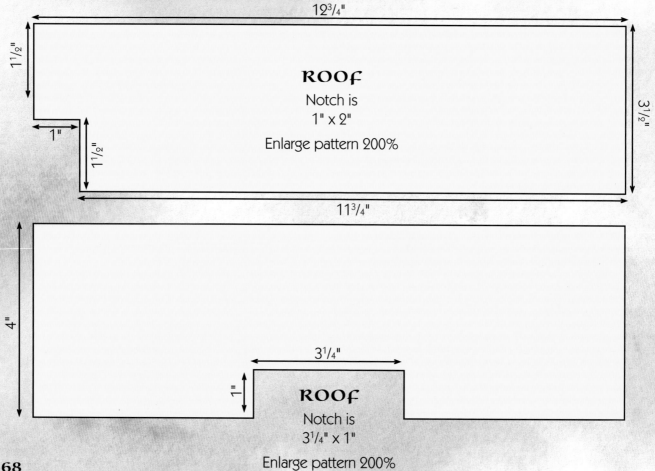

$12^3/_4$"

$1^1/_2$"

ROOF

Notch is
1" x 2"

Enlarge pattern 200%

$3^1/_2$"

1"

$1^1/_2$"

$11^3/_4$"

4"

$3^1/_4$"

1"

ROOF

Notch is
$3^1/_4$" x 1"

Enlarge pattern 200%

STARDUST INN

materials

Wood:
- ☐ Front, $9^3/_4$" x $5^1/_4$" x $^1/_2$"
- ☐ Back, $9^3/_4$" x $5^1/_4$" x $^1/_2$"
- ☐ Sides, $4^1/_4$" x $7^3/_8$" x $^1/_2$" (2)
- ☐ Base, $6^1/_4$" x $12^3/_4$" x $^1/_4$" (*)
- ☐ Roof, $11^3/_4$" x $3^1/_2$" x $^1/_2$" (*)
- ☐ Roof, $11^3/_4$" x 4" x $^1/_2$" (*)
- ☐ Two-story entry front,
      $3^1/_4$" x $7^7/_8$" x $^1/_2$"
- ☐ Two-story entry roof,
      $2^1/_2$" x $3^1/_8$" x $^1/_4$"
- ☐ Two-story entry roof,
      $2^3/_4$" x $3^3/_8$" x $^1/_4$"
- ☐ Dormer fronts,
      $1^1/_2$" x 2" x $^1/_4$" (2)
- ☐ Dormer sides,
      $1^1/_8$" x $1^1/_8$" x $^1/_4$" (2)
- ☐ Dormer roofs,
      $1^1/_4$" x $2^1/_2$" x $^1/_4$" (2)
- ☐ Dormer roofs,
      $1^1/_2$" x $2^3/_4$" x $^1/_4$" (2)

Balsa wood:
$^1/_8$" x 3" x 12"
$^1/_2$" x 1" x $11^3/_4$"

Turned posts:
Veranda corner posts,
   $^1/_4$" x $^1/_4$" x 6" (2)

Hardware, $^1/_{24}$ scale:
Door hinge assemblies (2)
Door knob

Trim:
Small gingerbread trim,
   $^1/_{16}$" x $^3/_8$" x 11"

Decorative accessories:
Dried flowers, tiny
Dried greenery, tiny

Paints & finishes:
Dark olive green, forest
   green, gray, and
   white acrylic paints
Matte acrylic spray

how-to

1. Before beginning, care-fully read General Instructions on pages 7-12.

2. Using a table saw, cut wood for front, back, and sides using basic cottage blueprints on page 117.

3. Cut wood for base and roof using altered dimensions given.

4. Cut wood for two-story entry front and roof using two-story entry patterns on page 126.

5. Cut wood for dormer fronts, sides, and roofs using dormer patterns on page 121.

6. Using graphite paper and a stylus, transfer door on front of angel house and on front of two-story entry using door placement pattern on page 73.

7. Using a jigsaw, cut out doors.

8. Cut a $3^1/_4$"-wide x 1" high notch centered along $11^3/_4$" edge of 4" roof to accom-modate two-story entry using notch placement patterns on page 73.

9. Using a craft knife, cut $^1/_8$"-thick balsa wood piece into doors using door pattern on page 73. Cut one solid door and one door with openings.

10. Cut $^1/_8$"-thick balsa wood into three 2"-wide x $^1/_2$"-high pieces, angling each end, for window boxes on two-story entry and dormers. Cut two $2^1/_2$"-wide x $^1/_2$"-high pieces, angling each end, for window boxes on front of angel house.

11. Cut $1/8$"-thick balsa wood into twelve $1/2$"-wide x $1^3/4$"-high pieces for shutters.

12. For balcony, cut a $3^1/4$"-wide x $1/2$"-high notch centered along $11^3/4$" edge of $1/2$"-thick balsa wood to accommodate two-story entry using notch placement patterns on page 73.

13. Using wood glue, assemble front, back, and sides of angel house and glue roof together. <u>Note: Do not glue roof on at this time.</u>

14. Assemble fronts and sides of dormers and glue dormer roofs together. <u>Note: Do not glue roofs on at this time, but bevel them at 45° angles to fit pitch of angel house roof.</u>

15. Glue assembled angel house on base, allowing $1^1/2$" in front, $1/2$" in back, and 1" on each side of base.

16. Glue two-story entry to front of angel house and on base using door placement pattern on page 73 for position and glue two-story entry roof together. <u>Note: Do not glue roof on at this time, but bevel it at a 45° angle to fit pitch of angel house roof.</u>

17. Using a paintbrush, paint angel house on the inside and the outside, two-story entry, fronts and sides of dormers, top side of angel house roof, top side of two-story entry roof, top sides of dormer roofs, balcony, including all outside edges, both sides of gingerbread trim, including all outside edges, veranda corner posts, and both sides of solid door, including all outside edges, with white acrylic paint.

18. Paint base, including all outside edges, all outside edges of two-story entry, underside of angel house roof, including all outside edges, underside of two-story entry roof, including all outside edges, underside of dormer roofs, including all outside edges, both sides of door with openings, including all outside edges, top and bottom of balcony, all window boxes and shutters, and a $5/8$" vertical stripe on each side of two-story entry front with dark olive green acrylic paint.

19. Paint one square window with a half-round window on top, including all cross members, on front of each dormer, on each side of two-story entry above balcony, and on upper portion of two-story entry above roof line with dark olive green using photograph on page 69 for placement.

Paint one square window, including all cross members, on each side of two-story entry below balcony. Make certain all second-floor windows are centered above first-floor windows.

20. Paint one half-round window, including all cross members, on two-story entry above balcony, centering window above door and making it slightly larger than others.

21. Paint two square windows with half-round windows on top, including all cross members, on back of angel house. Position windows for second-floor placement. Paint two square windows, including all cross members, centered underneath second-floor windows. Make certain tops of all windows are aligned.

22. Float-shade windows and cross members with gray acrylic paint.

23. Paint fishscale shingles on upper portion of each dormer above windows with gray using photograph for placement.

24. Float-shade louvres on shutters with forest green acrylic paint.

25. Using a ruler and a pencil, mark horizontal placement lines on angel house roof, two-story entry roof, and dormer roofs. Allow approximately ½" between each placement line.

26. Starting at bottom edges of roof lines and working across, float-shade scallops with gray for fishscale shingles. Alternate position of scallops on each row using photograph for placement.

27. Using wood glue, attach door with openings to solid door to make a single door.

28. Using a dremel tool, carefully attach door to front of angel house with door hinge assemblies.

29. Using industrial-strength glue, attach door knob to front side of door.

30. Using wood glue, attach roof on angel house. Attach beveled roof on two-story entry. Attach beveled roofs on dormers.

31. Glue dormers on roof using photograph for placement. Make certain windows on front of angel house are centered below windows on dormers.

32. Glue balcony across front of angel house using door placement pattern on page 73 for position.

33. Using a craft knife, cut gingerbread trim to fit across front and sides of balcony and glue in place.

34. Cut veranda corner posts to fit between balcony and base and glue in place using photograph for placement.

35. Glue 2"-wide window boxes below dormer windows and below window in upper portion of two-story entry.

36. Glue 2½"-wide window boxes below lower square windows on front of angel house.

37. Glue one shutter on each side of windows above balcony and on each side of windows on back of angel house.

38. Using graphite paper and a stylus, transfer saying to angel house using photograph for placement.

39. Using a lining brush, paint saying with dark olive green acrylic paint.

40. Seal angel house with matte acrylic spray.

41. Using craft glue, fill window boxes with dried flowers and greenery and make a wreath on front door.

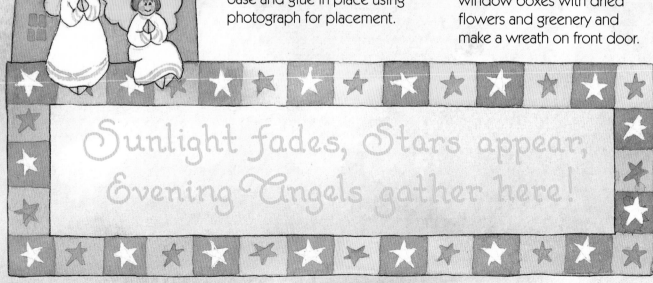

Sunlight fades, Stars appear, Evening Angels gather here!

Saying actual size

DOOR PLACEMENT PATTERN

DOOR PATTERN

FRONT
Doorway is
$1^7/_8$" x $2^1/_2$"

Enlarge pattern 200%

DOORS
Doorway is
$1^7/_8$" x $2^1/_2$"

Opening in
top of door
is $1^1/_2$" x 1"

Cut 1 Solid Door

Cut 1 Door with Openings

Pattern actual size

NOTCH PLACEMENT PATTERNS

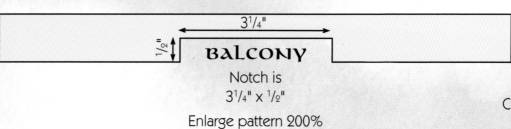

$3^1/_4$"

$^1/_2$"

BALCONY
Notch is
$3^1/_4$" x $^1/_2$"

Enlarge pattern 200%

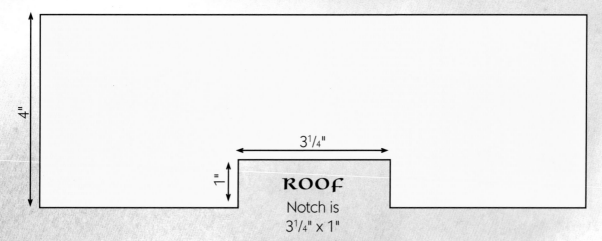

4"

$3^1/_4$"

1"

ROOF
Notch is
$3^1/_4$" x 1"

Enlarge pattern 200%

a sacred sanctuary

materials

Wood:
- ☐ Front, 9³/₄" x 5¹/₄" x ¹/₂"
- ☐ Back, 9³/₄" x 5¹/₄" x ¹/₂"
- ☐ Sides, 4¹/₄" x 7³/₈" x ¹/₂" (2)
- ☐ Base, 9" x 12³/₄" x ¹/₂" (*)
- ☐ Roof, 11³/₄" x 3¹/₄" x ¹/₂"
- ☐ Roof, 11³/₄" x 3³/₄" x ¹/₂"
- ☐ Vestibule front,
     2³/₄" x 5¹/₄" x ¹/₄"
- ☐ Vestibule sides,
     2" x 2³/₄" x ¹/₄" (2)
- ☐ Vestibule way roof,
     2⁵/₈" x 2¹/₂" x ¹/₄"
- ☐ Vestibule way roof,
     2⁵/₈" x 2³/₄" x ¹/₄"
- ☐ Steeple walls
     (front and back),
     1¹/₂" x 2¹/₂" x ¹/₄" (2)
- ☐ Steeple walls (side),
     1¹/₈" x 1⁷/₈" x ¹/₄" (2)
- ☐ Steeple roof,
     1¹/₄" x 2" x ¹/₄"
- ☐ Steeple roof,
     1¹/₂" x 2" x ¹/₄"

Balsa wood:
2" x 1⁷/₈" x ¹/₄"

Windows:
Sheets of glass:
  9¹/₂" X 5" (2), 1¹/₂" x 3" (2),
  1¹/₂" square

Siding:
Clapboard siding, ¹/₄"
  (3 sheets)

Hardware, ¹/₂₄ scale:
Door hinge assemblies (2)
Eye screw, ¹/₂"
Keyplate and door knob

Decorative accessories:
Wooden chimney,
  2" square x 3" high
Brass bell, ¹/₂"
Small gold chain, 1¹/₂"

Paints & finishes:
Dark gold, dark gray, and
  off-white acrylic paints
Blue, orange, purple, red,
  and yellow glass paints
Permanent gold marker
Texturizing gel
Matte acrylic spray

how-to

1. Before beginning, carefully read General Instructions on pages 7-12.

2. Note: This angel house has been rotated so the front and back become the sides and the sides become the front and back.

3. Using a table saw, cut wood for front, back, sides, and roof using basic cottage blueprints on page 117.

4. Cut wood for base using altered dimensions given and pattern on page 77.

5. Cut wood for vestibule front, sides, and roof using vestibule patterns on page 125.

6. Cut wood for steeple walls and roof using dimensions given and steeple patterns on page 78.

7. Using a jigsaw, cut a "V" in bottom of wooden chimney to fit over 45° angle pitch of angel house roof.

8. Using graphite paper and a stylus, transfer windows on sides of angel house and of vestibule and window and door on front of vestibule using window and door placement patterns on page 77.

9. Transfer openings in steeple walls using steeple patterns on page 78.

10. Using a drill and ¼" drill bit, drill pilot holes in each corner of windows and openings on steeple walls. Note: <u>All windows on sides of angel house and openings on steeple walls are arched at top. Windows on sides of vestibule are arched at top and bottom.</u>

11. Using a jigsaw, cut out windows, openings, and door. Save and set door aside.

12. Using wood glue, assemble front, back, and sides of angel house and glue roof together. Note: <u>Do not glue roof on at this time.</u>

Enlarge saying 155%

13. Glue assembled angel house on base, aligning back and sides with outside edges of base.

14. Assemble front and sides of vestibule and glue roof together. Note: Do not glue roof on at this time.

15. Glue assembled vestibule to front of angel house and on base.

16. Assemble steeple and glue roof together. Note: Do not glue roof on at this time.

17. Apply texturizing gel in a circular motion to outside walls of angel house, vestibule, steeple, and chimney according to manufacturer's directions. Note: Do not apply texturizing gel to top of chimney.

WINDOW AND DOOR PLACEMENT PATTERNS

SIDES

Windows are
$1\frac{1}{8}$" x $3\frac{3}{8}$"

Enlarge pattern 200%

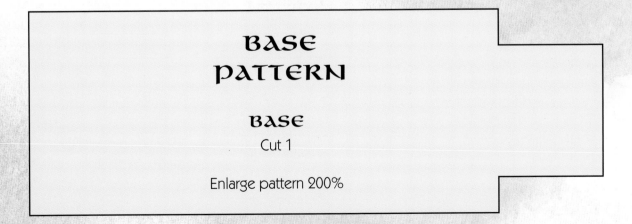

BASE PATTERN

BASE

Cut 1

Enlarge pattern 200%

18. Using a paintbrush, paint angel house, vestibule, and steeple on the inside with dark gold acrylic paint.

19. Paint outside walls of angel house, vestibule, steeple, and chimney with off-white acrylic paint.

20. Paint top of chimney with dark gray acrylic paint.

21. Spray angel house with matte acrylic spray.

22. Mix blue, orange, purple, red, and yellow glass paints together and randomly paint all sheets of glass to make stained glass windows.

23. Using industrial-strength glue, attach sheets of glass over appropriate windows inside angel house and vestibule.

24. Glue clapboard siding to angel house, vestibule, and steeple roofs for shingles. Leave a ¼" overhang on angel house roof only.

25. Using a paintbrush, wash roofs on tops, bottoms, and all outside edges and front door on front, back, and all outside edges, with dark gray acrylic paint.

26. Using a dremel tool, carefully attach door to front

of vestibule with door hinge assemblies.

27. Using industrial-strength glue, attach keyplate and door knob to front side of door.

28. Using a screwdriver, attach eye screw inside center of steeple roof. Hook chain to eye screw and brass bell to chain.

29. Using wood glue, attach

roofs to angel house, vestibule, and steeple. Glue steeple centered on top of chimney and glue chimney 1⅛" in from front edge of angel house roof.

30. Using graphite paper and a stylus, transfer saying on page 76 to sides of angel house using photograph for placement.

31. Using a permanent gold marker, write over saying.

STEEPLE PATTERNS

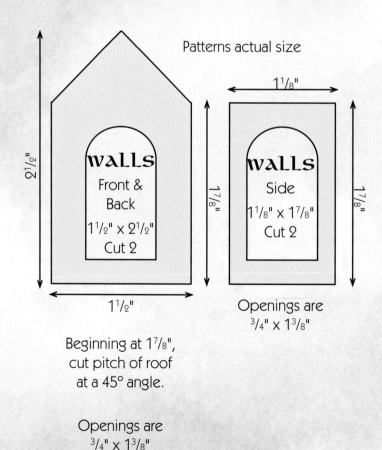

Patterns actual size

walls
Front & Back
1½" x 2½"
Cut 2

2½"

1⅞"

1½"

Beginning at 1⅞",
cut pitch of roof
at a 45° angle.

Openings are
¾" x 1⅜"

1⅛"

walls
Side
1⅛" x 1⅞"
Cut 2

1⅞"

Openings are
¾" x 1⅜"

Oh, Garden Angel
small and sweet
Before you enter,
Wipe your feet.

BETTER ANGEL
HOMES & GARDENS

BETTER ANGEL HOMES & GARDENS

materials

Wood:
- ☐ Front, $9^3/_4$" x $5^1/_4$" x $^1/_2$"
- ☐ Back, $9^3/_4$" x $5^1/_4$" x $^1/_2$"
- ☐ Sides, $4^1/_4$" x $7^3/_8$" x $^1/_2$" (2)
- ☐ Base, 6" x $10^3/_4$" x $^1/_2$" (*)
- ☐ Roof, $11^3/_4$" x $3^1/_2$" x $^1/_2$"
- ☐ Roof, $11^3/_4$" x 4" x $^1/_2$"
- ☐ Porch roof (Front),
   $10^1/_4$" x 2" x $^1/_4$"
- ☐ Porch roof (Back),
   $2^1/_4$" x $1^1/_2$" x $^1/_4$"
- ☐ Yard, $12^1/_4$" x $14^1/_4$" x $^1/_2$" (*)
- ☐ Chimney, $2^1/_4$" x $8^3/_4$" x 2"

Balsa wood:
$^1/_8$" x $^1/_4$" x 10"

Windows & doors, $^1/_{24}$ scale:
8-pane window frames,
   $1^1/_4$" x $2^3/_4$" (3)
Louvered shutters (6)
Scrap of white fabric
White lace, $^3/_4$"-wide x $^1/_4$ yard
Sheer pink ribbon,
   $1^1/_4$"-wide x $^1/_2$ yard
Traditional doors and frames,
   $1^1/_2$" x $3^1/_2$" (2)

Hardware, $^1/_{24}$ scale:
Gold-plated door knobs (2)

Shingles:
Fishscale shingles, $^3/_8$" x $^3/_4$"
   (approximately 700)

Decorative accessories:
Miniature bricks, 1 sheet
Lattice, 2"-wide x 9"
Window box, $3^1/_8$" x $^3/_8$" x $^1/_2$"
Pre-cut watering can, 3" x 3"

Embellishments, optional:
Miniature garden trellis
Miniature bench
Miniature flower cart
Miniature flower pots:
   $^3/_4$" (7), 1" (2)
Miniature garden spade
Small artificial flowers,
   assorted colors

Paints & finishes:
Dark blue, medium blue, dark green, light green, light rose, white, dark yellow, and medium yellow acrylic paints
Texturizing gel
Matte acrylic spray
White wash stain sealer

how-to

1. <u>Before beginning, carefully read General Instructions on pages 7-12.</u>

2. Using a table saw, cut wood for front, back, sides, and roof using basic cottage blueprints on page 117.

3. Cut wood for base using altered dimensions given.

4. Cut wood for porch roofs and yard using dimensions given.

5. Cut wood for chimney using the cottage chimney pattern on page 122.

6. Using graphite paper and a stylus, transfer windows and doors on front and back of angel house using window and door placement patterns on page 83.

7. Using a drill and 1/4" drill bit, drill pilot holes in each corner of windows.

8. Using a jigsaw, cut out windows and doors.

9. Cut a 1 1/2"-wide x 1/2" high notch 1/8" from edge of 3 1/2" roof to accommodate chimney using notch placement pattern on page 83.

10. Using a craft knife, cut 10" long balsa wood piece into porch supports for front and back porches.

11. Using a toothpick, apply wood glue around window and door frames and set them in place.

12. Assemble front, back, and sides of angel house and glue roof together. <u>Note: Do not glue roof on at this time.</u>

13. Glue assembled angel house on base, aligning back and sides with outside edges of base. Front of base will extend out to make a porch.

14. Glue chimney on left side of angel house.

15. Glue lattice on right side of angel house.

16. Glue front porch roof to angel house roof just underneath edge.

17. Starting at bottom edges of roof lines, glue shingles to angel house roof and both porch roofs. <u>Note: Back porch roof has not been attached to angel house yet.</u>

18. Mark angel house placement on yard and glue miniature bricks down for patio and front walk. Randomly glue clusters of bricks to angel house on outside walls.

19. Apply texturizing gel to outside walls of angel house and over yard according to manufacturer's directions. When desired thickness is achieved, lightly wipe texturizing gel off the bricks with a damp sponge.

20. Using a paintbrush, paint angel house on the inside with light rose acrylic paint.

21. Paint window and door frames and pre-cut watering can with medium blue acrylic paint. Float-highlight around watering can with dark blue acryic paint.

22. Paint yard with dark green acrylic paint.

23. Paint roof, shutters, and doors with dark yellow acrylic paint.

24. Paint porch and outside walls of angel house, including chimney, with light green acrylic paint.

25. Paint over bricks with a mixture of light rose and white acrylic paints.

26. Seal all painted surfaces with white wash stain sealer.

27. Using industrial-strength glue, attach fabric, white lace, and sheer pink ribbon to windows on inside of angel house to make curtains.

28. Using wood glue, attach roof on angel house.

29. Glue porch roof just above back door and glue porch supports in position on front and back porch roofs.

30. Glue angel house to yard.

31. Glue shutters and window box in position.

32. Using industrial-strength glue, attach door knobs to front sides of doors.

33. Using graphite paper and a stylus, transfer saying below to pre-cut watering

can using photograph for placement.

34. Using a lining brush, paint saying with medium yellow acrylic paint.

35. Glue watering can to angel house roof using photograph for placement.

36. Seal angel house with matte acrylic spray.

37. If desired, embellish yard around angel house with a miniature garden trellis, bench, flower cart, flower pots, garden spade, and an assortment of small artificial flowers.

Oh,
Garden Angel,
Small and sweet,
Before you enter
Wipe your feet.

WINDOW AND DOOR PLACEMENT PATTERNS

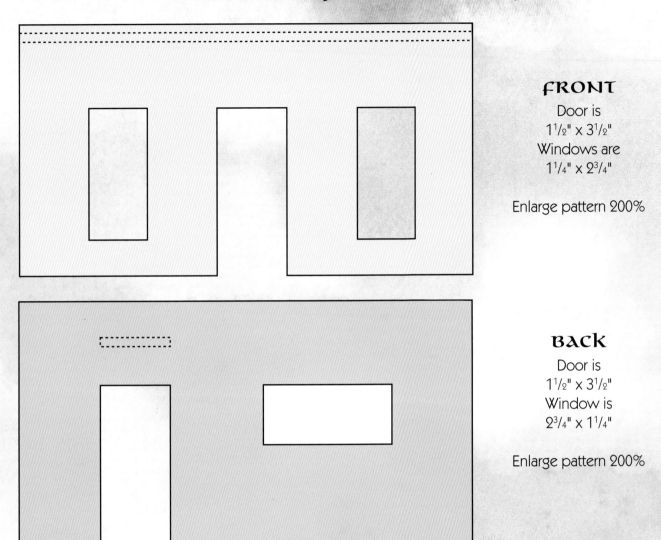

FRONT
Door is
$1^{1}/_{2}$" x $3^{1}/_{2}$"
Windows are
$1^{1}/_{4}$" x $2^{3}/_{4}$"

Enlarge pattern 200%

BACK
Door is
$1^{1}/_{2}$" x $3^{1}/_{2}$"
Window is
$2^{3}/_{4}$" x $1^{1}/_{4}$"

Enlarge pattern 200%

NOTCH PLACEMENT PATTERN

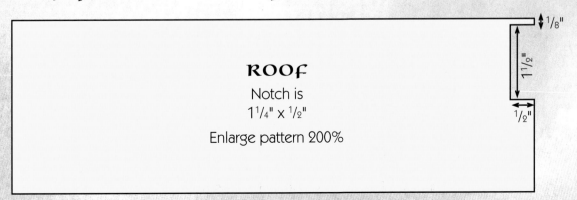

ROOF
Notch is
$1^{1}/_{4}$" x $^{1}/_{2}$"

Enlarge pattern 200%

$^{1}/_{8}$"

$1^{1}/_{2}$"

$^{1}/_{2}$"

Angels will cook
in this warm little nook.
If you don't believe,
don't bother to look.

A SWEET RETREAT

Materials

Wood:
- [ ] Front, 9³/₄" x 5¹/₄" x ¹/₂"
- [ ] Back, 9³/₄" x 5¹/₄" x ¹/₂"
- [ ] Sides, 4¹/₄" x 7³/₈" x ¹/₂" (2)
- [ ] Base, 6¹/₄" x 10³/₄" x ¹/₄" (*)
- [ ] Roof, 11³/₄" x 3¹/₄" x ¹/₂"
- [ ] Roof, 11³/₄" x 3³/₄" x ¹/₂"
- [ ] Entry way front,
     2³/₄" x 4¹/₄" x ¹/₂"
- [ ] Entry way sides,
     2" x 2⁷/₈" x ¹/₂" (2)
- [ ] Entry way roof,
     2³/₄" x 2¹/₂" x ¹/₂"
- [ ] Entry way roof,
     2³/₄" x 3" x ¹/₂"

Balsa wood:
¹/₄" x 2" x 6"

Windows:
Gingham cotton fabric, ¹/₃ yard
Coordinating thread

Hardware, ¹/₂₄ scale:
Door hinge assemblies (4)

Decorative accessories:
Wooden bow, 2"
Wooden cherries, ⁵/₈" (2)
Wooden rolling pins, 1¹/₂" (2)

Embellishments, optional:
Pie, painted
Woven basket
Red holly berry spray

Paints & finishes:
Cream, mustard, red, and
   tan acrylic paints
Golden oak stain
Liquid stain varnish
Liquid matte acrylic

Bread dough:
Loaf of sliced white bread
Craft glue
Cornstarch
Mixing bowl
Sealable plastic bags
Rolling pin

How-to

1. <u>Before beginning, carefully read General Instructions on pages 7-12.</u>

2. Using a table saw, cut wood for front, back, sides, and roof using basic cottage blueprints on page 117.

3. Cut wood for base using altered dimensions given.

4. Cut wood for entry way front, sides, and roof using entry way patterns on page 124.

5. Using graphite paper and a stylus, transfer windows and doors on front, back, one side, and entry way front using window and door placement patterns on pages 88-89.

6. Using a drill and ¹/₄" drill bit, drill pilot holes in each corner of windows. <u>Note: All windows are arched at top.</u>

7. Using a jigsaw, cut out windows and doors.

8. Using a craft knife, cut ¹/₄"-thick balsa wood piece into doors using window and door placement patterns.

85

17. Using a dremel tool, carefully attach doors to front and back of angel house with door hinge assemblies.

18. Using fabric scissors, cut fabric into five 4" x 4" squares.

19. Fold each fabric square in half and, using a needle and coordinating thread, gather-stitch along 4" side of all five fabric squares to make curtains.

20. Using industrial-strength glue, attach curtains to windows on inside of angel house.

21. Using wood glue, attach roof on angel house. Attach roof on entry way.

22. To make the dough to cover the angel house roof and the entry way roof and for the window trim, remove crust from slices of white bread.

23. Tear two bread slices into small pieces and place in a mixing bowl. Add 1 tablespoon craft glue.

24. Knead bread and craft glue into a ball. Sprinkle cornstarch on ball and continue kneading until ball is no longer sticky.

25. Place ball of dough in a sealable plastic bag.

9. Using wood glue, assemble front, back, and sides of angel house and glue roof together. Note: Do not glue roof on at this time.

10. Assemble front and sides of entry way and glue entry way roof together. Note: Do not glue roof on at this time.

11. Glue assembled entry way to front of angel house using photograph on page 84 for placement.

12. Stain base, including all outside edges, with golden oak stain according to manufacturer's directions.

13. Using a paintbrush, paint angel house and entry way on the inside and the outside with mustard acrylic paint.

14. Paint both sides of angel house roof, including all outside edges, and both sides of entry way roof, including all outside edges, with tan acrylic paint.

15. Paint both sides of doors, including all outside edges, wooden bow, wooden cherries, and rolling pin handles with red acrylic paint.

16. Paint rolling pins, door knobs, and a heart design on front of doors with cream acrylic paint.

26. Repeat process until all bread slices have been used and made into balls of dough.

27. For window trim on top and bottom of windows, form dough into 10 small balls similar in size. Form balls of dough into crescent shapes to fit width of windows. Pinch the edge of dough with fingers in three places.

28. Using a toothpick, add indents to resemble fork tines in a pie crust, then poke a series of small holes into dough.

29. Using craft glue, glue trim on top and bottom of windows.

30. For window trim on sides of windows, form dough into two ropes. Using a table knife, cut ropes of dough to fit height of windows.

31. Glue ropes on sides of windows.

32. Using a rolling pin, roll out enough dough to cover one side of angel house roof and glue in place.

33. Repeat process for remaining side of angel house roof and for both sides of entry way roof.

34. Cover all outside edges of angel house roof with dough and glue in place.

35. For roof trim, form dough into crescent shapes to fit width and height of angel house roof and entry way roof. Pinch the edge of dough with fingers along edges.

36. Using a toothpick, add indents to resemble fork tines in a pie crust, then poke a series of small holes into dough.

37. Glue trim around outside perimeter of and across top of angel house roof and entry way roof.

38. Form dough into ropes. Using a table knife, cut ropes of dough to fit width and height of angel house roof.

39. Glue ropes inside existing trim around outside perimeter of angel house roof.

40. Allow dough to dry thoroughly; two to three days is recommended.

41. Using a paintbrush, paint all dried dough with tan acrylic paint.

42. Using craft glue, attach one wooden cherry centered on top of angel house roof and one wooden cherry centered on top of entry way roof.

43. Using a paintbrush, apply liquid stain varnish to angel house roof, entry way roof, and window trim

according to manufacturer's directions.

44. Using craft glue, attach wooden rolling pins above windows on front of angel house and wooden bow above front door using photograph for placement.

45. Using wood glue, glue assembled angel house and entry way on base, aligning back and sides with outside edges of base.

46. Using graphite paper and a stylus, transfer saying on page 89 to angel house roof using photograph for placement.

47. Using a lining brush, paint saying with red acrylic paint.

48. Seal angel house with liquid matte acrylic.

49. Allow liquid acrylic to dry thoroughly.

50. If desired, a pie can be glued inside one of the front windows and a woven basket filled with red holly berries can be glued near the entry way.

WINDOW AND DOOR PLACEMENT PATTERNS

SIDE
One Side Only

Window is
1 1/8" x 1 7/8"

Enlarge pattern 200%

ENTRY WAY FRONT

Doorway is
1 1/2" x 2 1/4"

Pattern actual size

WINDOW AND DOOR PLACEMENT PATTERNS (CONTINUED)

FRONT

Windows are
1$\frac{1}{2}$" x 2$\frac{1}{2}$"

Enlarge pattern 200%

BACK

Windows are
1$\frac{1}{8}$" x 1$\frac{7}{8}$"

Doorway is
1$\frac{1}{2}$" x 3"

Enlarge pattern 200%

Angels will cook
in this warm little nook.
If you don't believe,
don't bother to look.

Saying actual size

hamburger haven

materials

Wood:
- Front, $9^3/_4$" x $5^1/_4$" x $^1/_2$"
- Back, $9^3/_4$" x $5^1/_4$" x $^1/_2$"
- Sides,
    $4^1/_4$" x $5^1/_4$" x $^1/_2$" (2) (*)
- Base, $9^1/_2$" x $10^3/_4$" x $^1/_4$" (*)
- Roof, $10^3/_4$" x $4^1/_4$" x $^1/_4$" (*)

Balsa wood:
$^1/_4$" x 5" x 3"
$^1/_4$" x $^1/_4$" x 36"

Windows & door, $^1/_{24}$ scale:
Windows, $2^{25}/_{32}$" x $1^9/_{32}$" (7)
French doors, $2^5/_8$" x $3^{13}/_{16}$"

Siding:
Clapboard siding,
    $^1/_2$" (2 sheets)

Decorative accessories:
Silver-tone knife, $2^1/_2$"
Silver-tone fork, $2^1/_2$"
Silver-tone fork charm, 1"
Silver-tone spoon charm, 1"
Silver-tone clock button, $^1/_2$"
Checkered paper, 3" x 6"
Lightweight cardboard, 2" x 5"
Wooden dowels,
    $^1/_8$"-diameter x $3^3/_4$" long (2)

Paints & finishes:
Black, gray, metallic gold,
    metallic silver, red, and
    white acrylic paints
Faux granite spray paint
Satin acrylic spray

how-to

1. <u>Before beginning, carefully read General Instructions on pages 7-12.</u>

2. Using a table saw, cut wood for front and back using basic cottage blueprints on page 117.

3. Cut wood for sides and roof using altered dimensions given.

4. Cut wood for base using base pattern on page 94.

5. Using wood glue, attach clapboard siding to front, back, and sides. Allow a $^1/_2$" overlap on each end of front and back to cover width of wood on sides once front, back, and sides have been assembled. Also allow a $^1/_4$" overlap on top to accommodate roof.

6. Using graphite paper and a stylus, transfer windows on front, back, and sides and door on front using window and door placement patterns on pages 93-94.

7. Using a drill and $^1/_4$" drill bit, drill pilot holes in each corner of windows.

8. Using a jigsaw, cut out windows and door.

9. Using a craft knife, cut $^1/_4$"-thick balsa wood piece into sign using sign pattern on page 94.

10. Using wood glue, assemble front, back, and sides of angel house. <u>Note: Do not glue roof on at this time.</u>

11. Spray-paint base, including all outside edges, with faux granite spray paint according to manufacturer's directions.

12. Using a paintbrush, paint angel house on the inside, clapboard siding, both sides of roof, including all outside edges, both sides of balsa wood sign, and ⅛"-diameter wooden dowels with metallic silver acrylic paint.

13. Paint both sides of french doors, including all outside edges, door frame, window frames, all outside edges of balsa wood sign, clapboard siding (fourth from bottom), and ¼"-square balsa wood for roof trim with red acrylic paint.

14. Using wood glue, carefully attach door frame to front of angel house.

15. Using pliers, bend 1" fork and spoon charms for door handles.

16. Using industrial-strength glue, attach door handles to front side of doors.

Saying actual size

ANGELS DINE HERE

17. Using a toothpick, apply wood glue around window frames and set them in place.

18. Using wood glue, attach roof on angel house.

19. Using a craft knife, miter ¼"-square balsa wood to fit around outside perimeter of roof and glue in place.

20. Glue assembled angel house on base, aligning back and sides with outside edges of base.

21. Using graphite paper and a stylus, transfer saying above to sign using photograph for placement.

22. Using a lining brush, paint saying with red, black, gray, white, and metallic gold acrylic paints.

23. Using wood glue, attach sign to front of angel house using window and door placement patterns on page 93 for position.

24. Using industrial-strength glue, attach clock button to top of sign.

25. Using rubber cement, adhere checkered paper to lightweight cardboard, wrapping paper underneath and trimming as needed with craft scissors.

26. Using a paintbrush, paint underside of cardboard with black acrylic paint.

27. When paint is dry, slightly bend cardboard to make an awning.

28. Using craft glue, adhere awning to bottom of sign using photograph for placement.

29. Glue wooden dowels between awning and base using photograph for placement.

30. Glue 2½" knife and fork to wooden dowels.

31. Seal angel house with satin acrylic spray.

WINDOW AND DOOR PLACEMENT PATTERNS

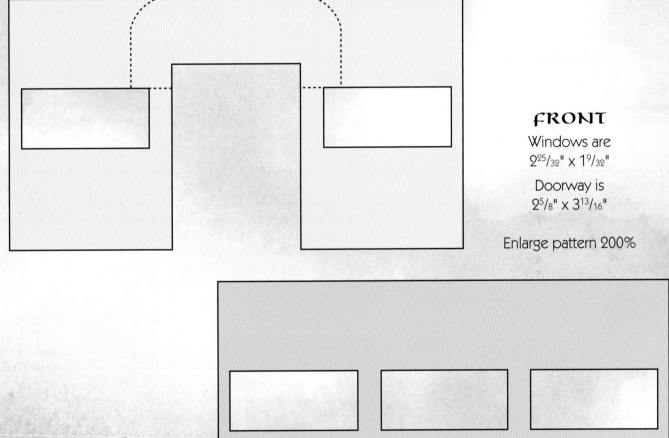

FRONT
Windows are
$2^{25}/_{32}$" x $1^{9}/_{32}$"

Doorway is
$2^{5}/_{8}$" x $3^{13}/_{16}$"

Enlarge pattern 200%

BACK
Windows are
$2^{25}/_{32}$" x $1^{9}/_{32}$"

Enlarge pattern 200%

WINDOW AND DOOR PLACEMENT PATTERNS (CONTINUED)

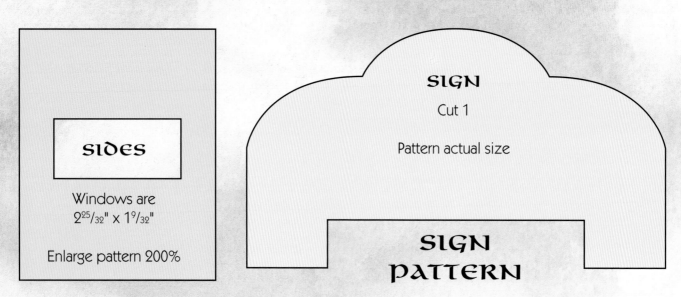

SIDES

Windows are
$2^{25}/_{32}$" x $1^9/_{32}$"

Enlarge pattern 200%

SIGN

Cut 1

Pattern actual size

SIGN PATTERN

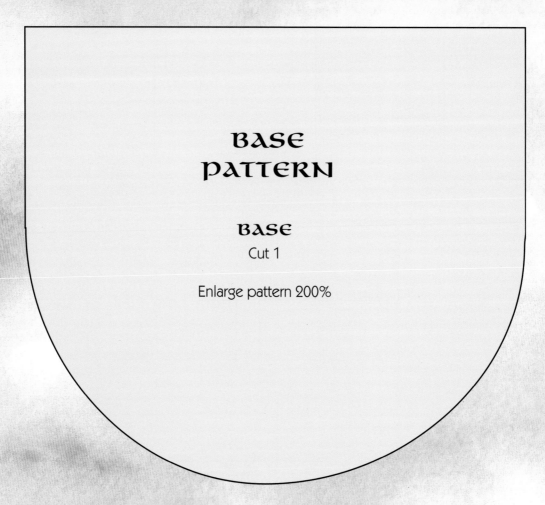

BASE PATTERN

BASE

Cut 1

Enlarge pattern 200%

HOME ON THE RANGE

THIS RUSTIC OLD HOUSE WHERE ANGELS ABIDE

HAS PLENTY OF LOVE TO SHARE INSIDE

WELCOME

HOME ON THE RANGE

MATERIALS

Wood:
☐ Front, 12" x 12³/₄" x ¹/₄"
☐ Back, 12" x 12³/₄" x ¹/₄"
☐ Sides, 6" x 15³/₄" x ¹/₄" (2)
☐ Base, 9" x 12¹/₂" x ¹/₄" (*)
☐ Roof, 15" x 5" x ¹/₄"
☐ Roof, 15" x 5¹/₄" x ¹/₄"
☐ Porch roof, 12¹/₂" x 3¹/₈" x ¹/₄"

Balsa wood:
¹/₈" x ¹/₂" x 2¹/₄"
¹/₄" x 3" x 36"
³/₈" x ³/₈" x 12¹/₂"
¹/₃₂" x 3" x 36" (2 sheets)

Windows:
Screen scraps, 5" x 10"

Hardware:
Door hinge assemblies, ¹/₂" (2)
Eye screw, ¹/₄"
Nail, tiny

Paints & finishes:
Burnt umber, grey-tan,
  off-white acrylic paints
Crackle medium
Top soil, dried
Matte acrylic spray

HOW-TO

1. <u>Before beginning, carefully read General Instructions on pages 7-12.</u>

2. Using a table saw, cut wood for front, back, sides, and roof using basic two-story blueprints on page 118.

3. Cut wood for base using altered dimensions given.

4. Cut wood for porch roof using dimensions given.

5. Using graphite paper and a stylus, transfer windows on front and back and door on front using window and door placement patterns on page 98.

6. Using a drill and ¹/₄" drill bit, drill pilot holes in each corner of windows.

7. Using a jigsaw, cut out windows and door. Save and set door aside.

8. Using a craft knife, cut ¹/₄"-thick balsa wood into fourteen 2¹/₄"-long x ¹/₂"-wide pieces for trim above and below windows and fourteen 2³/₄"-long x ¹/₂"-wide pieces for trim at each side of windows. Remove small pieces of balsa wood from both edges of window trim pieces so they appear rustic and worn and measure approximately ¹/₄" to ¹/₂".

9. Cut ¹/₄"-thick balsa wood into two 7¹/₂"-long x ¹/₂"-wide pieces for porch posts. Remove small pieces of balsa wood from both edges of porch posts so they appear rustic and worn and measure approximately ³/₈" to ¹/₂".

10. Cut $1/4$"-thick balsa wood into one $1\frac{1}{8}$"-long x $3/8$"-wide piece, one $2\frac{3}{4}$"-long x $3/8$"-wide piece, and one $5\frac{1}{2}$"-long x $3/8$"-wide piece for porch railings. Remove small pieces of balsa wood from both edges of porch railings so they appear rustic and worn and measure approximately $1/16$" to $1/8$".

11. Cut ends of $1/8$"-thick balsa wood to make a sign with jagged ends. Set sign aside.

12. Break $1/32$"-thick balsa wood sheets into 1"-wide x 15"-long pieces for shingles on roof and 1"-wide x $12\frac{1}{2}$"-long pieces for shingles on porch roof.

13. Using wood glue, assemble front, back, and sides of angel house and glue roof together. <u>Note: Do not glue roof on at this time.</u>

14. Glue assembled angel house on base, aligning back and sides with outside edges of base.

15. Using a paintbrush, paint angel house on the inside and the outside, base, including all outside edges, both sides of angel house roof and porch roof, including all outside edges, both sides of door, including all outside edges, and all balsa wood pieces, including shingles, with grey-tan acrylic paint.

16. While paint is still slightly wet, gently rub dried top soil over all painted surfaces, except on angel house, for a rustic appearance. Remove excess dirt.

17. Apply crackle medium over acrylic paint on outside of angel house according to manufacturer's directions.

18. Paint over crackle medium with off-white acrylic paint that has been slightly thinned with water according to manufacturer's directions.

19. Using a dremel tool, carefully attach door to front of angel house with door hinge assemblies.

20. Attach eye screw to front side of door for door knob.

21. Using craft scissors, cut screen into seven $2\frac{1}{2}$" x $2\frac{1}{2}$" squares.

22. Using industrial-strength glue, attach screens to windows on inside of angel house. Fray some edges and leave unattached for a rustic appearance.

23. Gently rub dried top soil over outside of angel house for a rustic appearance. Remove excess dirt.

24. Using wood glue, attach roof on angel house.

25. Glue window trim around windows.

26. Glue $3/8$"-square balsa wood porch roof support across front of angel house using window and door placement pattern on page 98 for position.

27. Glue porch posts to base and glue porch railing to porch posts using photograph on page 95 for placement.

28. Glue porch roof on top of porch roof support and porch posts.

29. Starting at bottom edges of roof lines, glue shingles to roof and porch roof. Place shingles unevenly for a rustic appearance.

30. Using coarse sandpaper, lightly sand front, back, and sides of angel house. Remove excess dust.

31. Using graphite paper and a stylus, transfer saying below to angel house using photograph for placement.

32. Using a lining brush, paint saying with burnt umber acrylic paint. Paint "WELCOME" on sign for door with burnt umber.

33. Using a dremel tool, carefully attach sign to door with nail.

34. Seal angel house with matte acrylic spray.

THIS RUSTIC OLD HOUSE WHERE ANGELS ABIDE HAS PLENTY OF LOVE TO SHARE INSIDE

Enlarge saying 125%

WINDOW AND DOOR PLACEMENT PATTERNS

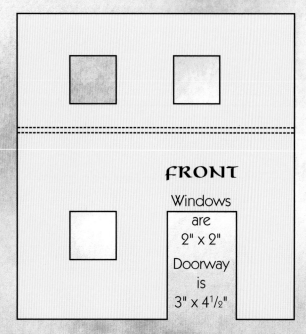

FRONT

Windows are 2" x 2"

Doorway is 3" x 4½"

Enlarge pattern 400%

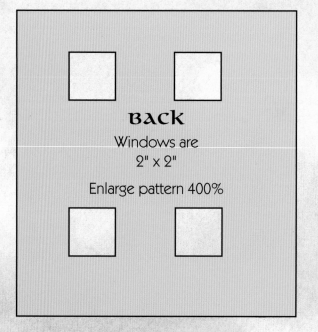

BACK

Windows are 2" x 2"

Enlarge pattern 400%

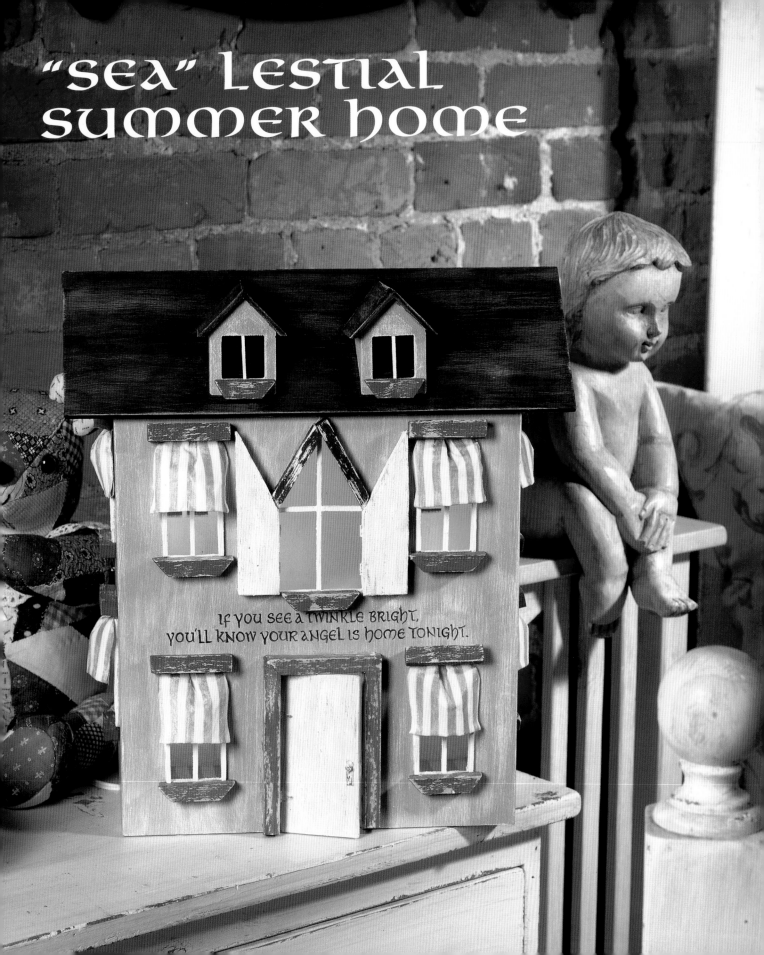

"SEA" LESTIAL SUMMER HOME

IF YOU SEE A TWINKLE BRIGHT,
YOU'LL KNOW YOUR ANGEL IS HOME TONIGHT.

"sea" Lestial summer home

materials

Wood:
- ☐ Front, 12" x 12³/₄" x ¹/₄"
- ☐ Back, 12" x 12³/₄" x ¹/₄"
- ☐ Sides, 6" x 15³/₄" x ¹/₄" (2)
- ☐ Base, 6" x 12¹/₂" x ¹/₄"
- ☐ Roof, 15" x 5" x ¹/₄"
- ☐ Roof, 15" x 5¹/₄" x ¹/₄"

Balsa wood:
¹/₈" x ¹/₈" x 36" (4)
³/₈" x ³/₈" x 36"
¹/₂" x ¹/₂" x 36" (3)
¹/₂" x 4" x 5"

Windows, ¹/₂₄ scale:
Dormers,
    2¹/₂" x 3" x 1⁵/₈" (2)
Striped cotton fabric, ¹/₃ yard
Aluminum foil
Paper towel tube
Fabric stiffener
Plastic bag

Hardware, ¹/₂₄ scale:
Door hinge assemblies (6)
Keyplate and door knob

Paints & finishes:
Dark blue, light blue,
    medium blue, light gray,
    dark green, and
    white acrylic paints
Matte acrylic spray

how-to

1. <u>Before beginning, carefully read General Instructions on pages 7-12.</u>

2. Using a table saw, cut wood for front, back, sides, base, and roof using basic two-story blueprints on page 118.

3. Using graphite paper and a stylus, transfer windows on front, back, and sides and door on front using window and door placement patterns on page 102.

4. Using a drill and ¹/₄" drill bit, drill pilot holes in each corner of windows.

5. Using a jigsaw, cut out windows and door. Save and set door aside.

6. Using a craft knife, cut ¹/₂"-square balsa wood into twelve 2¹/₄"-long pieces for trim above windows and thirteen 2¹/₄"-long pieces, angling each end, for window boxes. Cut two 1³/₄"-long pieces, angling each end, for window boxes at bottom of dormers. Cut one 3¹/₂"-long piece and two 5¹/₈"-long pieces for door frame.

7. Cut ¹/₂"-thick balsa wood into two 1¹/₄" x 4³/₄" pieces for shutters. Beginning at 2¹/₂", angle one end on both pieces.

8. Cut ³/₈"-square balsa wood into one 2³/₄"-long piece and one 2¹/₂"-long piece for trim above center window, angling one end on both pieces to fit angle on shutters.

9. Cut ¹/₈"-square balsa wood into pieces for window frames and pieces for cross members.

10. Using wood glue, assemble front, back, and sides of angel house and glue roof together. <u>Note: Do not glue roof on at this time.</u>

11. Glue assembled angel house on base, aligning front,

back, and sides with outside edges of base.

12. Using a paintbrush, paint angel house on the outside, base, including all outside edges, and dormers on the outside with light blue acrylic paint.

13. Paint both sides of roof, including all outside edges, both sides of dormer roofs, including all outside edges, and trim above center window with dark blue and dark green acrylic paints.

14. Paint angel house on the inside, dormers on the inside, both sides of door and shutters, including all outside edges, window frames, and cross members with white acrylic paint.

15. Paint remaining balsa wood pieces with medium blue acrylic paint.

16. Dry-brush angel house on the outside and base, including all outside edges, with white.

17. Dry-brush both sides of door and shutters, including all outside edges, with light gray acrylic paint.

18. Using coarse sandpaper, sand edges of roof lines and all medium blue colored balsa wood pieces to randomly remove some paint for a weathered appearance. Remove excess dust.

19. Using a dremel tool, carefully attach door to front of angel house with door hinge assemblies. Attach one shutter on each side of center window. Note: Hinges on shutters are decorative and are not intended to be functional.

20. Using industrial-strength glue, attach keyplate and door knob to front side of door.

21. Using wood glue, attach window frames to each side of $1^{1}/_{2}$" x $3^{3}/_{8}$" windows. Glue cross members in position using photograph on page 99 for placement.

22. Using fabric scissors, cut fabric, with stripes going vertically, into twelve $2^{1}/_{2}$" x $4^{5}/_{8}$" strips.

23. Place aluminum foil around a paper towel tube and pour fabric stiffener into a plastic bag.

24. Dip fabric strips in fabric stiffener and remove. Fold each fabric strip in half, flatten, and place around paper towel tube.

25. Allow fabric to dry thoroughly and become stiff to make curtains. Note: Fabric will become stiff, but should remain pliable.

26. Remove folded fabric strips from paper towel tube.

27. Repeat process until all fabric strips have been used.

28. Cut corners off curtains at raw edge.

Enlarge saying 140%

IF YOU SEE A TWINKLE BRIGHT, YOU'LL KNOW YOUR ANGEL IS HOME TONIGHT.

29. Make two pleats in center of each curtain and, using industrial-strength glue, attach curtains to windows on outside of angel house.

30. Using wood glue, attach roof on angel house.

31. Glue dormers on roof using photograph for placement.

32. Glue window trim above 1$\frac{1}{2}$" x 3$\frac{3}{8}$" windows and window boxes below 1$\frac{1}{2}$" x 3$\frac{3}{8}$" windows.

33. Glue window trim at an angle above and window box below center window. Glue window boxes at bottom of each dormer.

34. Glue door frame in place.

35. Using graphite paper and a stylus, transfer saying on page 101 to angel house using photograph for placement.

36. Using a lining brush, paint saying with dark blue acrylic paint.

37. Seal angel house with matte acrylic spray.

WINDOW AND DOOR PLACEMENT PATTERNS

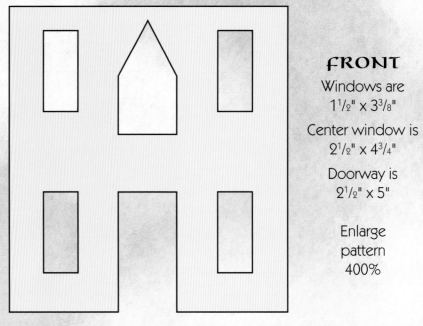

FRONT
Windows are
1$\frac{1}{2}$" x 3$\frac{3}{8}$"

Center window is
2$\frac{1}{2}$" x 4$\frac{3}{4}$"

Doorway is
2$\frac{1}{2}$" x 5"

Enlarge
pattern
400%

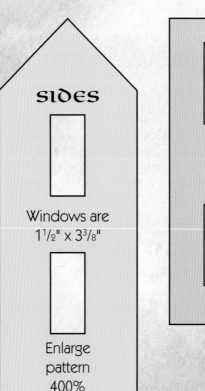

SIDES

Windows are
1$\frac{1}{2}$" x 3$\frac{3}{8}$"

Enlarge
pattern
400%

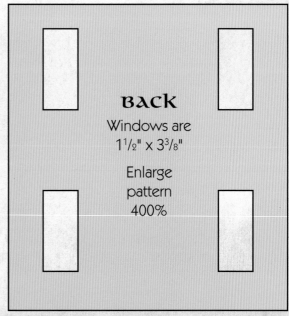

BACK
Windows are
1$\frac{1}{2}$" x 3$\frac{3}{8}$"

Enlarge
pattern
400%

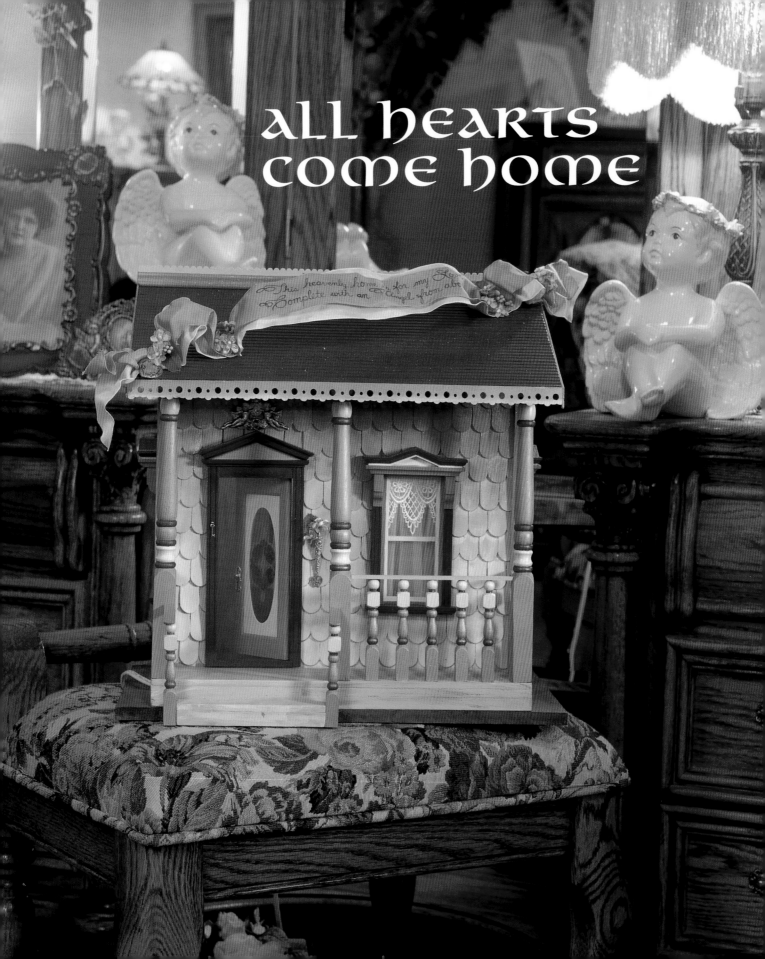

ALL HEARTS
COME HOME

all hearts come home

materials

Wood:
- [ ] Front, 12" x 12³/₄" x ¹/₄"
- [ ] Back, 12" x 12³/₄" x ¹/₄"
- [ ] Sides, 6" x 14¹/₄" x ¹/₄" (2) (*)
- [ ] Base, 12" x 16" x ¹/₂" (*)
- [ ] Porch, 13" x 3" x 1"
- [ ] Front step, 5" x 1" x ³/₄"
- [ ] Roof, 15" x 6" x ¹/₄" (*)
- [ ] Roof, 15" x 7³/₄" x ¹/₄" (*)

Balsa wood:
¹/₈" x ¹/₂" x 24"
¹/₈" x 3" x 6"

Turned posts:
Porch posts, ³/₄" x ³/₄" x 13" (3)
Newel posts,
   ⁷/₁₆" x ⁷/₁₆" x 3¹/₂" (11)

Windows & door, ¹/₁₂ scale:
Victorian windows,
   2⁹/₁₆" x 5¹/₁₆" (3)
Victorian side-by-side
   window, 5¹/₁₆" x 5¹/₁₆"
Glass, 3" x 3" (2)
White sheer fabric, ¹/₄ yard
White Victorian lace,
   3"-wide x ¹/₂ yard
Coordinating thread
Victorian door with
   oval window and frame,
   3¹/₁₆" x 7⁷/₁₆"
Victorian etched door pane
   insert, to fit oval in door

Hardware, ¹/₁₂ scale:
Keyplate and door knob
Skeleton key
Nail, tiny

Siding, shingles, moulding & trim:
Clapboard siding, ¹/₄"
   (4 sheets)
Fishscale shingles, ²³/₃₂" x 1¹/₄"
   (approximately 800)
Fancy Victorian trim,
   ¹/₁₆" x ¹¹/₁₆" x 24" (4)
Corner moulding,
   ¹/₂" x ¹/₂" x 24" (4)
Roof ridge moulding,
   ⁹/₁₆" x 1¹/₁₆" x 22"

Decorative accessories:
Wire-edged rose ribbon,
   1¹/₂"-wide x 1 yard
Wire-edged pink ribbon,
   2"-wide x 1 yard
Cherub charm, 1¹/₂"
Double cherub charm, 2¹/₂"
Filigree charm, 2"
Heart charm, ¹/₂"
Heart charms, ³/₄" (2)
Silk flowers, tiny

Embellishments, optional:
Beaded suncatchers
Topiary trees (2)

Paints & finishes:
Burgundy, dark green,
   dark rose, green,
   light rose, rose, and
   white acrylic paints
Peach, purple, and
   red glass paints
Pearl glaze spray

how-to

1. Before beginning, carefully read General Instructions on pages 7-12.

2. Using a table saw, cut wood for front and back using basic two-story blueprints on page 118.

3. Cut wood for base, sides, and roof using altered dimensions given. Beginning at 12^3/$_4$", cut pitch of roof at a 25° angle.

4. Cut wood for porch and front step using dimensions given.

5. Using a miter saw, miter one long end of each roof piece at a 65° angle.

6. Using graphite paper and a stylus, transfer windows on front, back, and sides and door on front using window and door placement patterns on page 108.

7. Using a drill and ^{1}/$_4$" drill bit, drill pilot holes in each corner of windows and door.

8. Using a jigsaw, cut out windows and door.

9. Using a craft knife, round both ends of the ^{1}/$_8$"-thick (x ^{1}/$_2$" x 24") balsa wood.

10. Enlarge attic window pattern to allow an additional

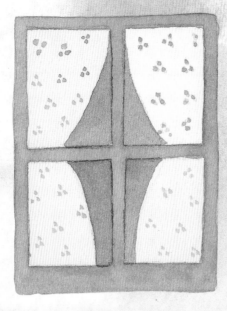

^{1}/$_4$" around all sides. Using a craft knife, cut ^{1}/$_8$"-thick (x 3" x 6") balsa wood into two hearts. Cut centers from hearts, ^{1}/$_4$" from outside edges, for trim around attic windows.

11. Using wood glue, assemble front, back, and sides of angel house. Note: Do not glue roof on at this time.

12. Glue assembled angel house on base, allowing 3" in front and in back and 1" on each side.

13. Glue clapboard siding to roof for shingles.

14. Using a ruler and a pencil, mark horizontal placement lines around outside perimeter of angel house. Allow approximately 1" between each placement line.

15. Starting at bottom edges of angel house and working across, glue shingles for "gingerbread" siding to front, back, and sides, leaving 1" in front without shingles to accommodate porch.

16. Using a craft knife, trim shingles around window and door openings.

17. Using a paintbrush, paint first two bottom rows of gingerbread siding on angel house with white acrylic paint. Add light rose, rose, and dark rose acrylic paints accordingly with each two new rows of gingerbread siding to graduate paint from white at bottom to dark rose at top using photographs on pages 103-104 for placement.

18. Paint both sides of roof, including all outside edges, with burgundy acrylic paint.

19. Paint both sides of fancy Victorian trim with rose.

20. Paint both sides of roof ridge moulding with rose. Accent top decorative edge with light rose.

21. Paint corner moulding with rose.

22. Remove windows from window frames. Paint door frame and window frames with light rose, rose, dark rose, and burgundy using photographs for placement.

23. Paint porch and front step with rose, then dry-brush with light rose.

24. Paint balsa wood hearts with burgundy.

25. Paint balsa wood with rounded ends for porch railing with rose.

26. Paint porch posts and newel posts with rose. Accent decorative turnings with light rose and dark rose.

27. Paint both sides of door with rose. Accent inset with oval window with light rose.

Enlarge saying 165%

28. Paint angel house on the inside with dark rose. Paint floor on the inside with burgundy.

29. Paint base, including all outside edges, with dark green acrylic paint, then dry-brush with green acrylic paint.

30. Replace windows in window frames.

31. Paint back side of etched door pane insert with glass paints using photographs for placement. Mix red with peach to make pink. Mix red with purple to make burgundy.

32. Mix peach, purple, and red glass paints. Paint in swirls on both pieces of glass.

33. Allow glass paint to dry overnight.

34. Using wood glue, carefully attach door frame to front of angel house.

35. Using industrial-strength glue, attach keyplate and door knob to front side of door.

36. Glue etched door pane insert in position on door.

37. Using a toothpick, apply wood glue around window frames and set them in place.

38. Using industrial-strength glue, adhere glass to inside of angel house over openings for attic windows.

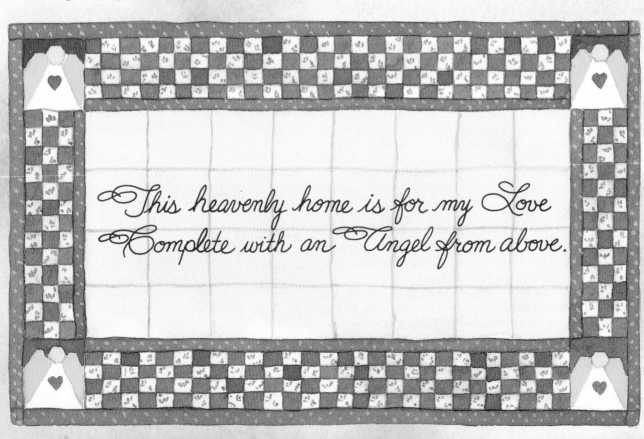

This heavenly home is for my Love Complete with an Angel from above.

39. Using fabric scissors, cut lace into three 2³/₄" pieces and one 5¹/₄" piece. Cut fabric into three 3³/₄" x 5¹/₄" pieces and one 7¹/₄" x 5¹/₄" piece.

40. Using a needle and coordinating thread, gather-stitch along 3³/₄" side of three fabric pieces and along 7¹/₄" side of remaining fabric piece.

41. Using industrial-strength glue, attach lace to windows on inside of angel house for valances.

42. If desired, beaded suncatchers can be glued to windows on inside of angel house between valances and sheer drapes.

43. Glue gathered fabric to windows on inside of angel house for sheer drapes.

44. Using wood glue, attach roof on angel house.

45. Using a craft knife, cut fancy Victorian trim to fit around roof and glue in place.

46. Cut roof ridge moulding to fit along top of roof and glue in place.

47. Glue porch on base in front of angel house, aligning at each side.

48. Glue front step to porch and outside edge of base, aligning bottoms of front step and base using photograph on page 103 for placement.

49. Glue corner moulding on corners of angel house. Using a craft knife, trim corner moulding to fit around porch.

50. Cut top of each porch post at a 60° angle to fit between roof and porch and glue in place using photograph for placement.

51. Glue newel posts to porch, evenly spaced between porch posts in front of angel house and evenly spaced between porch posts and house on each side.

52. Glue one newel post to each side of front step at front edge, aligning bottoms of newel post and front step.

53. Using a craft knife, cut ¹/₈"-thick (x ¹/₂" x 24") balsa wood to fit for porch railing and glue in place. Begin with each rounded end for hand railing between porch posts and newel posts on front step.

54. Glue heart trim around attic windows.

55. Using industrial-strength glue, attach double cherub charm centered above door.

56. Glue filigree charm to right of door and glue one ¹/₂" heart charm to bottom of filigree charm. Glue a few silk flowers into top opening of filigree charm.

57. Seal angel house with pearl glaze spray.

58. Using a dremel tool, carefully attach nail to door frame and hang skeleton key on nail.

59. Using graphite paper and a stylus, transfer saying on page 106 to center of 1¹/₂"-wide rose ribbon.

60. Using a lining brush, paint saying with dark rose acrylic paint.

61. Place 1½"-wide rose ribbon on top of 2"-wide pink ribbon and pinch together 3" from each end. Using a hot glue gun and glue sticks, secure each "pinched" end to opposite roof corners allowing ribbons to cascade across roof.

62. Repeat process by pinching ribbons together 3" from first pinched sections and securing in place.

63. Carefully position ribbons so saying can be read.

64. Hot-glue silk flowers on top of rose ribbon at pinched sections.

65. Hot-glue one ¾" heart charm on top of rose ribbon at opposite roof corners.

66. Hot-glue cherub charm on top of rose ribbon at center.

67. If desired, embellish outside of angel house with topiary trees placed on each side of side-by-side window at back of angel house.

WINDOW AND DOOR PLACEMENT PATTERNS

FRONT
Window is
2⁹/₁₆" x 5¹/₁₆"

Doorway is
3¹/₁₆" x 7⁷/₁₆"

Enlarge pattern 400%

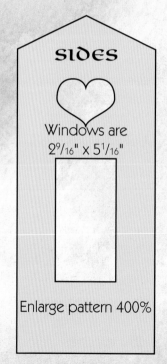

SIDES
Windows are
2⁹/₁₆" x 5¹/₁₆"

Enlarge pattern 400%

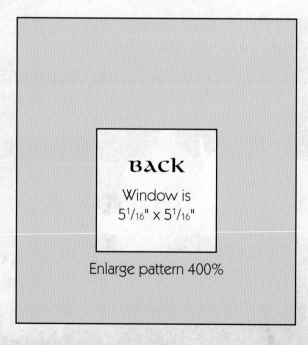

BACK
Window is
5¹/₁₆" x 5¹/₁₆"

Enlarge pattern 400%

MAJESTIC MANSION

The Christmas spirit will abide
As loving Angels are heard inside.

MAJESTIC MANSION

materials

Wood:
☐ Front, 18" x 9¹/₄" x ¹/₂"
☐ Back, 18" x 9¹/₄" x ¹/₂"
☐ Sides, 5³/₄" x 9¹/₄" x ¹/₂" (2)
☐ Base, 5³/₄" x 19" x ¹/₂"
☐ Front step, 11" x 1" x ¹/₂"
☐ Roof, 8³/₄" x 19¹/₂" x ¹/₂"

Balsa wood:
¹/₂" x ¹/₂" x 9¹/₄" (4)

Windows & doors, ¹/₂₄ scale:
Windows, 1⁹/₃₂" x 2²⁵/₃₂" (19)
Shutters, ¹/₂" X 2¹/₂" (24)
Glass, 2" x 2"
Light yellow sheer ribbon,
    1¹/₄"-wide x 3 yards
Traditional door and frame,
    1¹/₂" x 3¹/₂"
Yorktown door and frame,
    1¹¹/₁₆" x 3²³/₃₂"

Hardware, ¹/₂₄ scale:
Door knob
Keyplate and door knob

Siding & moulding:
Clapboard siding, ³/₈"
    (6 sheets)
Dentil crown moulding,
    ⁵/₁₆" x ⁷/₁₆" x 18" (6)
Corner moulding,
    ¹/₂" x ¹/₂" x 24" (4)
Wood filler

Embellishments, optional:
Christmas decorations
Christmas lights, tiny

Paints & finishes:
Black, medium yellow, and
    off-white acrylic paints
Matte acrylic spray

Enlarge saying 165%

how-to

1. Before beginning, carefully read General Instructions on pages 7-12.

2. Using a table saw, cut wood for base, front, back, sides, and roof using basic mansion blueprints on page 119.

3. Cut wood for front step using dimensions given.

4. Using wood glue, attach clapboard siding to front, back, and sides, overlapping bottom edges ¹/₂" to cover base once angel house is assembled.

The Christmas spirit will abide
As loving Angels are heard inside.

5. Using graphite paper and a stylus, transfer windows and doors on front, back, and sides using window and door placement patterns on page 112.

6. Using a drill and ¼" drill bit, drill pilot holes in each corner of windows and doors.

7. Using a jigsaw, cut out windows and doors.

8. Using wood glue, assemble front, back, and sides of angel house. <u>Note: Do not glue roof on at this time.</u>

9. Glue assembled angel house on base by placing base inside ½" clapboard siding overlap.

10. Using a miter saw, miter dentil crown moulding at 45° angles to fit around outside perimeter of roof.

11. Glue dentil crown moulding around roof.

12. If necessary, fill space between dentil crown moulding and roof line with wood filler. Allow wood filler to dry thoroughly and lightly sand using fine sandpaper.

13. Using a paintbrush, paint clapboard siding with medium yellow acrylic paint.

14. Paint both sides of roof and both sides of dentil crown

moulding with off-white acrylic paint.

15. Paint door frames, window frames, front step, and corner moulding with off-white.

16. Paint balsa wood pieces for porch posts with off-white.

17. Paint both sides of doors and shutters with black acrylic paint.

18. Paint angel house on the inside with medium yellow.

19. Using wood glue, carefully attach door frames to front and back of angel house.

20. Using industrial-strength glue, attach keyplate and door knob to front side of front door. Attach door knob to front side of back door.

21. Using fabric scissors, cut sheer ribbon into thirty-eight 2¾" lengths.

22. For each window, place two lengths of sheer ribbon on top of each other and slide into window frames between wooden panes and glass. Press glass over ribbon to secure.

23. Using a toothpick, apply wood glue around window frames and set them in place.

24. Glue one shutter on each side of windows on front and sides of angel house.

25. Using industrial-strength glue, adhere glass to inside of angel house over opening for round window.

26. Using wood glue, attach roof on angel house. Position roof so there is a ¾" overhang on each side, a 1" overhang in the back, and a 2" overhang in the front at center.

27. Glue front step, centered, on front of angel house.

28. Glue corner moulding on corners of angel house.

29. Glue porch posts between roof and front step using photograph on page 109 for placement.

30. Using graphite paper and a stylus, transfer saying on page 110 to angel house using photograph for placement.

31. Using a lining brush, paint saying with black acrylic paint.

32. Seal angel house with matte acrylic spray.

33. If desired, embellish outside of angel house with Christmas decorations and use tiny Christmas lights inside to light.

WINDOW AND DOOR PLACEMENT PATTERNS

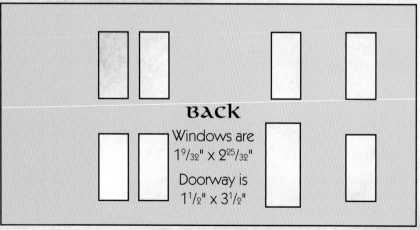

FRONT
Windows are
$1^9/_{32}$" x $2^{25}/_{32}$"

Round window is
$1^1/_2$" in diameter

Doorway is
$1^{11}/_{16}$" x $3^{23}/_{32}$"

Enlarge pattern 400%

SIDES
Windows are
$1^9/_{32}$" x $2^{25}/_{32}$"

Enlarge pattern 400%

BACK
Windows are
$1^9/_{32}$" x $2^{25}/_{32}$"

Doorway is
$1^1/_2$" x $3^1/_2$"

Enlarge pattern 400%

AROUND A CORNER AND NOT VERY FAR,
YOU THOUGHT YOU SAW A TWINKLING STAR.

DON'T BE FOOLED BY THIS BRIGHT LITTLE LIGHT,
'TIS ONLY AN ANGEL BEGINNING HER FLIGHT;

ON HER WAY TENDING THINGS,
THAT MEAN AS MUCH AS THE GIFTS SHE BRINGS;

WITH BLESSINGS, KINDNESS, AND
        THOUGHTFULNESS TOO,
THIS ANGEL HAS COME TO WATCH OVER YOU.

THAT WARM FUZZY PLACE WITHIN YOUR HEART,
IS ONLY A HOME FOR HER IN PART;

FOR WHEN THIS MESSENGER STOPS TO SING,
IN AN ANGEL HOUSE, SHE'LL REST HER WINGS.

A SPECIAL PLACE FOR HER ALONE;
SOMEWHERE RIGHT, TO CALL HER HOME.

FOR ANGELS HAVE HEARTS, BIG AS THE MOON,
THAT HELP US CHASE AWAY OUR GLOOM.

QUIETLY, THEY COME WITH THEIR GIFT OF LOVE,
FOR SOMEONE SPECIAL JUST NEEDING A HUG.

SO IN RETURN, YOU'LL WANT TO DUST AND KEEP
A LITTLE HOUSE WHERE YOUR ANGEL SLEEPS.

BASIC STUDIO BLUEPRINTS

FRONT
$5^{1}/_{2}$" x $3^{5}/_{8}$" x $^{1}/_{4}$"
Cut 1

Enlarge pattern 200%

BACK
$5^{1}/_{2}$" x $3^{5}/_{8}$" x $^{1}/_{4}$"
Cut 1

Enlarge pattern 200%

BASE
6" x $6^{1}/_{4}$" x $^{1}/_{4}$"
Cut 1

Enlarge pattern 200%

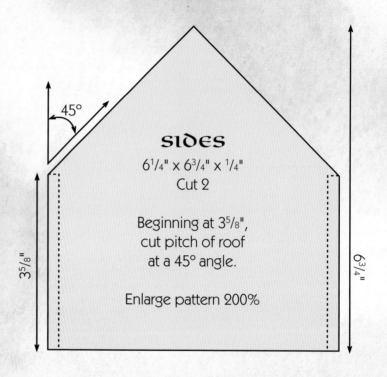

SIDES
$6^{1}/_{4}$" x $6^{3}/_{4}$" x $^{1}/_{4}$"
Cut 2

Beginning at $3^{5}/_{8}$",
cut pitch of roof
at a 45° angle.

Enlarge pattern 200%

45°

$3^{5}/_{8}$"

$6^{3}/_{4}$"

ROOF
$7^{1}/_{2}$" x $4^{3}/_{4}$" x $^{1}/_{4}$"
Cut 1
$7^{1}/_{2}$" x 5" x $^{1}/_{4}$"
Cut 1

Enlarge pattern 200%

BASIC ONE-STORY BLUEPRINTS

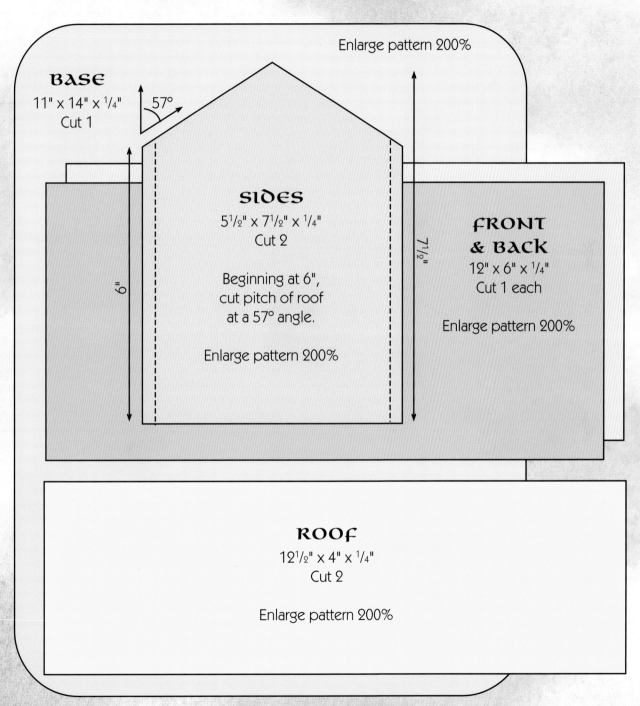

Enlarge pattern 200%

BASE
11" x 14" x ¼"
Cut 1

57°

SIDES
5½" x 7½" x ¼"
Cut 2

Beginning at 6",
cut pitch of roof
at a 57° angle.

Enlarge pattern 200%

6"

7½"

FRONT & BACK
12" x 6" x ¼"
Cut 1 each

Enlarge pattern 200%

ROOF
12½" x 4" x ¼"
Cut 2

Enlarge pattern 200%

BASIC HOUSE BLUEPRINTS

FRONT
8" x 7" x ¹/₂"
Cut 1

Enlarge pattern 400%

BACK
8" x 7" x ¹/₂"
Cut 1

Enlarge pattern 400%

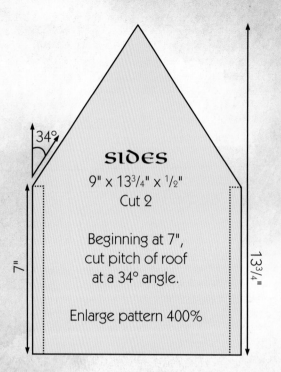

34°

SIDES
9" x 13³/₄" x ¹/₂"
Cut 2

Beginning at 7",
cut pitch of roof
at a 34° angle.

Enlarge pattern 400%

7"

13³/₄"

BASE
9" x 9" x ¹/₂"
Cut 1

Enlarge pattern 400%

ROOF
12" x 9" x ¹/₄"
Cut 2

Enlarge pattern 400%

BASIC COTTAGE BLUEPRINTS

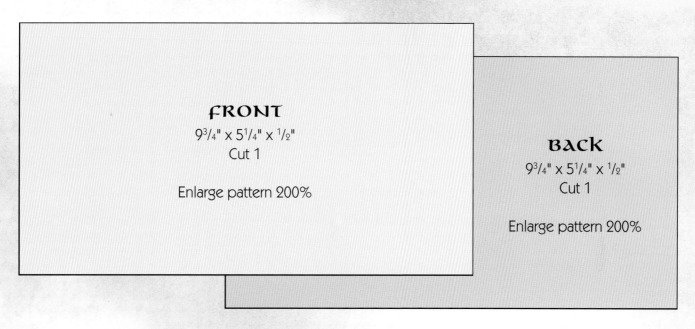

FRONT
$9^3/_4$" x $5^1/_4$" x $^1/_2$"
Cut 1

Enlarge pattern 200%

BACK
$9^3/_4$" x $5^1/_4$" x $^1/_2$"
Cut 1

Enlarge pattern 200%

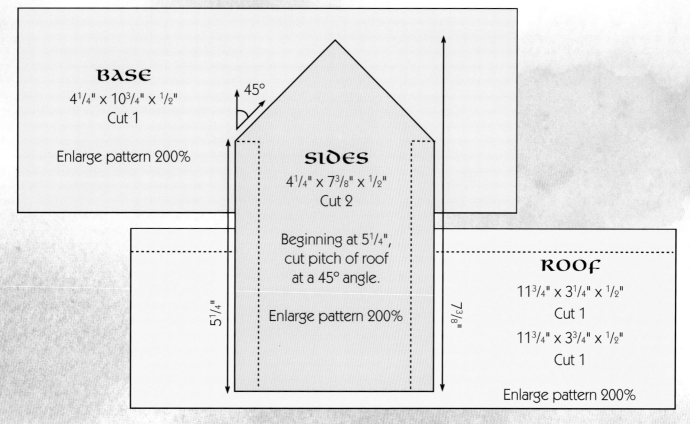

BASE
$4^1/_4$" x $10^3/_4$" x $^1/_2$"
Cut 1

Enlarge pattern 200%

45°

SIDES
$4^1/_4$" x $7^3/_8$" x $^1/_2$"
Cut 2

Beginning at $5^1/_4$",
cut pitch of roof
at a 45° angle.

Enlarge pattern 200%

$5^1/_4$"

$7^3/_8$"

ROOF
$11^3/_4$" x $3^1/_4$" x $^1/_2$"
Cut 1
$11^3/_4$" x $3^3/_4$" x $^1/_2$"
Cut 1

Enlarge pattern 200%

BASIC TWO-STORY BLUEPRINTS

FRONT
12" x 12³/₄" x ¹/₄"
Cut 1

Enlarge pattern 400%

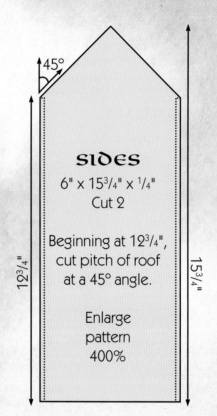

SIDES
6" x 15³/₄" x ¹/₄"
Cut 2

Beginning at 12³/₄",
cut pitch of roof
at a 45° angle.

Enlarge
pattern
400%

45°

12³/₄"

15³/₄"

ROOF
15" x 5" x ¹/₄"
Cut 1

15" x 5¹/₄" x ¹/₄"
Cut 1

Enlarge
pattern
400%

BACK
12" x 12³/₄" x ¹/₄"
Cut 1

Enlarge pattern 400%

BASE
6" x 12¹/₂" x ¹/₄"
Cut 1

Enlarge pattern 400%

BASIC MANSION BLUEPRINTS

FRONT
18" x 9¼" x ½"
Cut 1

Enlarge pattern 400%

BASE
5¾" x 19" x ½"
Cut 1

Enlarge
pattern
400%

BACK
18" x 9¼" x ½"
Cut 1

Enlarge pattern 400%

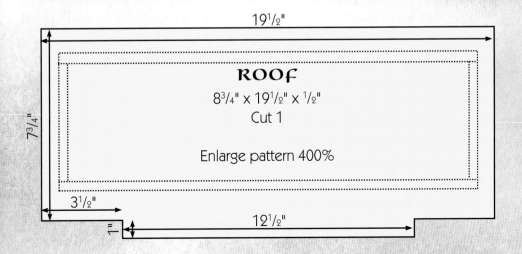

19½"

ROOF
8¾" x 19½" x ½"
Cut 1

Enlarge pattern 400%

7¾"

3½"

1"

12½"

SIDES
5¾" x 9¼" x ½"
Cut 2

Enlarge
pattern
400%

BELL TOWER PATTERNS

ROOF
4" x 3½" x ¼"
Cut 2

Pattern actual size

WALLS
Front & Back
3" x 6" x ¼"
Cut 2

Beginning at 4",
cut pitch of roof
at a 34° angle.

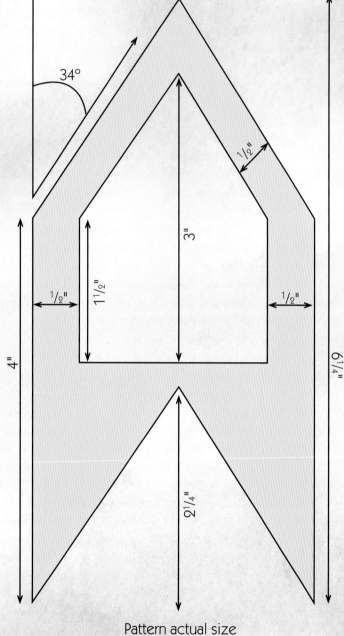

34°

½"

½"

1½"

3"

½"

4"

6¼"

2¼"

Pattern actual size

Once assembled, inside edges
at bottom must be beveled at
a 34° angle to fit pitch of roof.

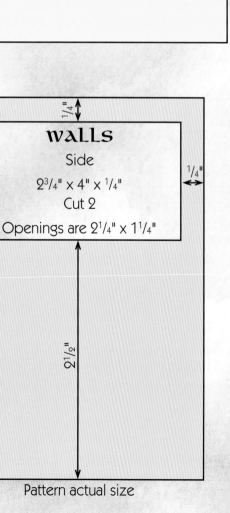

¼"

WALLS
Side
2¾" x 4" x ¼"
Cut 2

Openings are 2¼" x 1¼"

¼"

¼"

2½"

Pattern actual size

DORMER PATTERNS

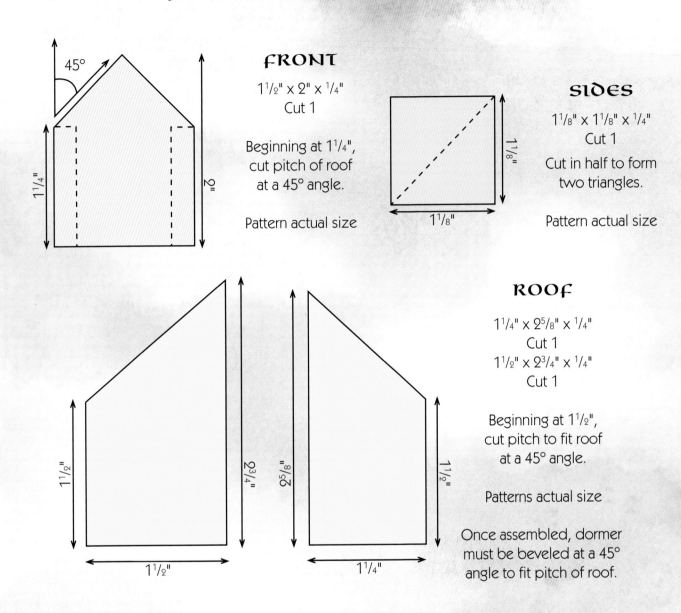

FRONT

$1\frac{1}{2}$" x 2" x $\frac{1}{4}$"
Cut 1

Beginning at $1\frac{1}{4}$",
cut pitch of roof
at a 45° angle.

Pattern actual size

SIDES

$1\frac{1}{8}$" x $1\frac{1}{8}$" x $\frac{1}{4}$"
Cut 1

Cut in half to form
two triangles.

Pattern actual size

ROOF

$1\frac{1}{4}$" x $2\frac{5}{8}$" x $\frac{1}{4}$"
Cut 1
$1\frac{1}{2}$" x $2\frac{3}{4}$" x $\frac{1}{4}$"
Cut 1

Beginning at $1\frac{1}{2}$",
cut pitch to fit roof
at a 45° angle.

Patterns actual size

Once assembled, dormer
must be beveled at a 45°
angle to fit pitch of roof.

chimney patterns

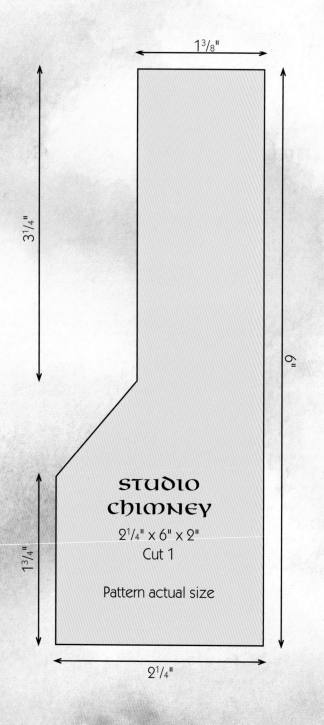

1³/₈"

3¹/₄"

6"

studio chimney

2¹/₄" x 6" x 2"
Cut 1

Pattern actual size

1³/₄"

2¹/₄"

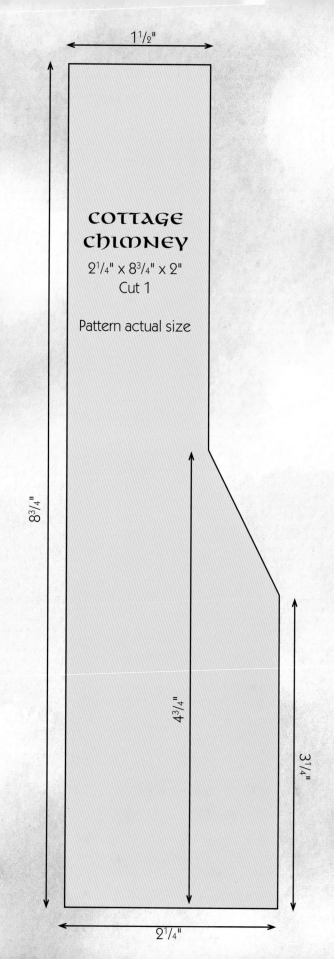

1¹/₂"

cottage chimney

2¹/₄" x 8³/₄" x 2"
Cut 1

Pattern actual size

8³/₄"

4³/₄"

3¹/₄"

2¹/₄"

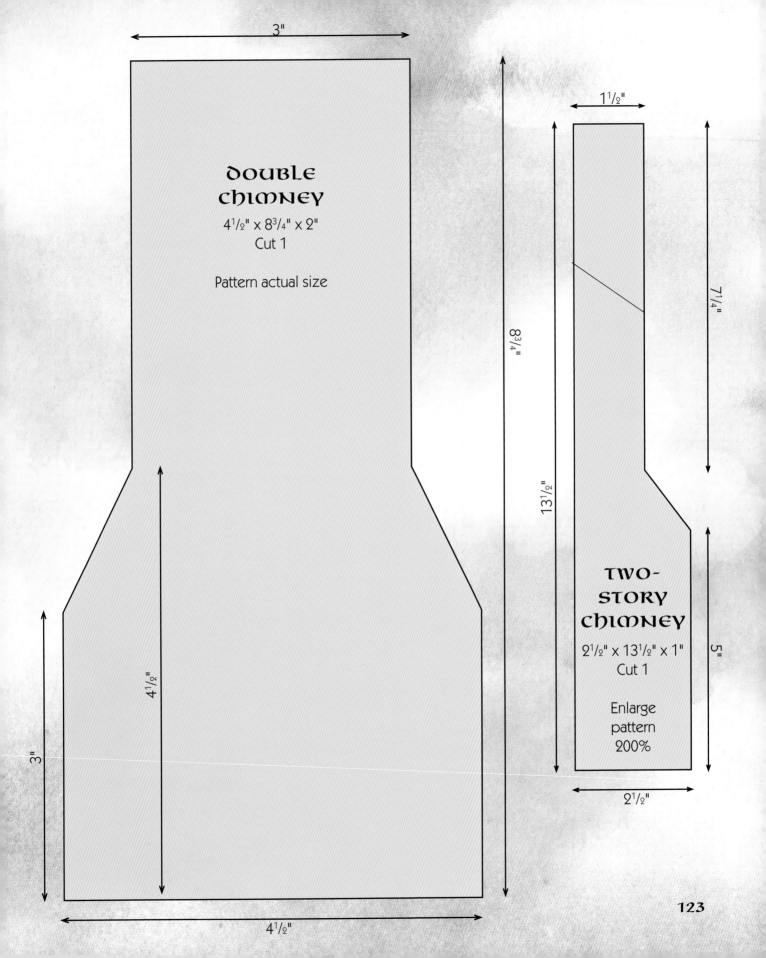

3"

DOUBLE CHIMNEY

$4^1/_2$" × $8^3/_4$" × 2"

Cut 1

Pattern actual size

$8^3/_4$"

$4^1/_2$"

3"

$4^1/_2$"

$1^1/_2$"

$7^1/_4$"

$13^1/_2$"

TWO-STORY CHIMNEY

$2^1/_2$" × $13^1/_2$" × 1"

Cut 1

Enlarge pattern 200%

5"

$2^1/_2$"

ENTRY WAY PATTERNS

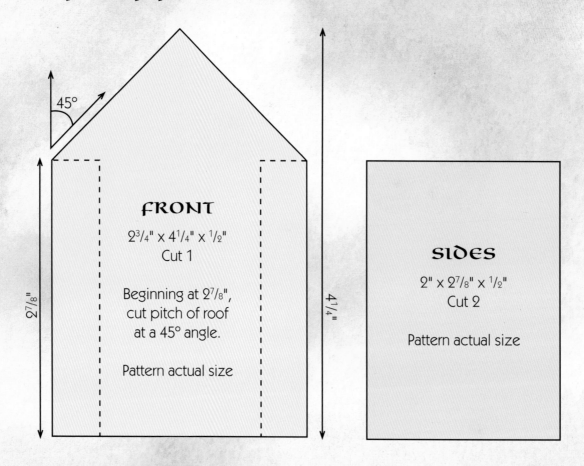

45°

FRONT

$2^3/_4$" x $4^1/_4$" x $^1/_2$"
Cut 1

Beginning at $2^7/_8$",
cut pitch of roof
at a 45° angle.

Pattern actual size

$2^7/_8$"

$4^1/_4$"

SIDES

2" x $2^7/_8$" x $^1/_2$"
Cut 2

Pattern actual size

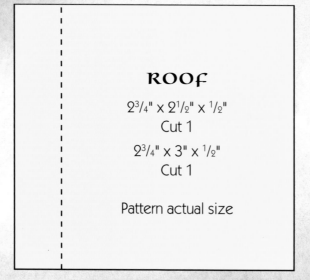

ROOF

$2^3/_4$" x $2^1/_2$" x $^1/_2$"
Cut 1

$2^3/_4$" x 3" x $^1/_2$"
Cut 1

Pattern actual size

124

VESTIBULE PATTERNS

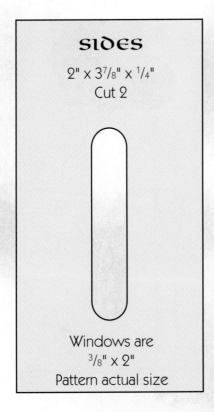

SIDES

2" x 3⁷/₈" x ¹/₄"

Cut 2

Windows are
³/₈" x 2"

Pattern actual size

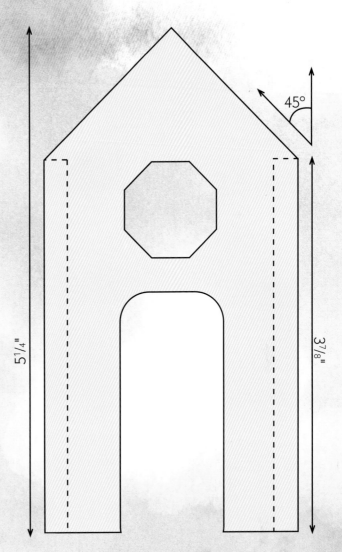

45°

5¹/₄"

3⁷/₈"

ROOF

2³/₄" x 2¹/₂" x ¹/₄"
Cut 1

2³/₄" x 2 ³/₄" x ¹/₄"
Cut 1

Pattern actual size

FRONT

2³/₄" x 5¹/₄" x ¹/₄"
Cut 1

Doorway is
1¹/₈" x 2¹/₂"

Octagonal Window is
1" x 1"

Beginning at 3⁷/₈",
cut pitch of roof
at a 45° angle.

Pattern actual size

TWO-STORY ENTRY PATTERNS

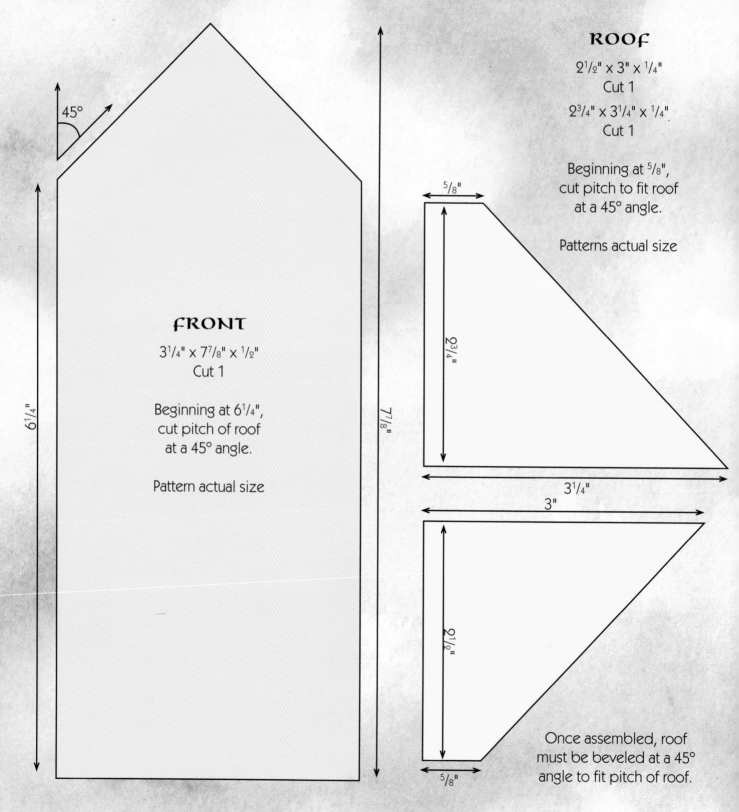

45°

ROOF

$2^{1}/_{2}$" x 3" x $^{1}/_{4}$"
Cut 1

$2^{3}/_{4}$" x $3^{1}/_{4}$" x $^{1}/_{4}$"
Cut 1

Beginning at $^{5}/_{8}$",
cut pitch to fit roof
at a 45° angle.

Patterns actual size

FRONT

$3^{1}/_{4}$" x $7^{7}/_{8}$" x $^{1}/_{2}$"
Cut 1

Beginning at $6^{1}/_{4}$",
cut pitch of roof
at a 45° angle.

Pattern actual size

$^{5}/_{8}$"

$2^{3}/_{4}$"

$6^{1}/_{4}$"

$7^{7}/_{8}$"

$3^{1}/_{4}$"

3"

$2^{1}/_{2}$"

$^{5}/_{8}$"

Once assembled, roof
must be beveled at a 45°
angle to fit pitch of roof.

126

METRIC CONVERSIONS

INCHES TO MILLIMETRES AND CENTIMETRES

INCHES	MM	CM	INCHES	CM	INCHES	CM
1/8	3	0.9	9	22.9	30	76.2
1/4	6	0.6	10	25.4	31	78.7
3/8	10	1.0	11	27.9	32	81.3
1/2	13	1.3	12	30.5	33	83.8
5/8	16	1.6	13	33.0	34	86.4
3/4	19	1.9	14	35.6	35	88.9
7/8	22	2.2	15	38.1	36	91.4
1	25	2.5	16	40.6	37	94.0
1 1/4	32	3.2	17	43.2	38	96.5
1 1/2	38	3.8	18	45.7	39	99.1
1 3/4	44	4.4	19	48.3	40	101.6
2	51	5.1	20	50.8	41	104.1
2 1/2	64	6.4	21	53.3	42	106.7
3	76	7.6	22	55.9	43	109.2
3 1/2	89	8.9	23	58.4	44	111.8
4	102	10.2	24	61.0	45	114.3
4 1/2	114	11.4	25	63.5	46	116.8
5	127	12.7	26	66.0	47	119.4
6	152	15.2	27	68.6	48	121.9
7	178	17.8	28	71.1	49	124.5
8	203	20.3	29	73.7	50	127.0

YARDS TO METRES

YARDS	METRES	YARDS	METRES	YARDS	METRES	YARDS	METRES	YARDS	METRES
1/8	0.11	2 1/8	1.94	4 1/8	3.77	6 1/8	5.60	8 1/8	7.43
1/4	0.23	2 1/4	2.06	4 1/4	3.89	6 1/4	5.72	8 1/4	7.54
3/8	0.34	2 3/8	2.17	4 3/8	4.00	6 3/8	5.83	8 3/8	7.66
1/2	0.46	2 1/2	2.29	4 1/2	4.11	6 1/2	5.94	8 1/2	7.77
5/8	0.57	2 5/8	2.40	4 5/8	4.23	6 5/8	6.06	8 5/8	7.89
3/4	0.69	2 3/4	2.51	4 3/4	4.34	6 3/4	6.17	8 3/4	8.00
7/8	0.80	2 7/8	2.63	4 7/8	4.46	6 7/8	6.29	8 7/8	8.12
1	0.91	3	2.74	5	4.57	7	6.40	9	8.23
1 1/8	1.03	3 1/8	2.86	5 1/8	4.69	7 1/8	6.52	9 1/8	8.34
1 1/4	1.14	3 1/4	2.97	5 1/4	4.80	7 1/4	6.63	9 1/4	8.46
1 3/8	1.26	3 3/8	3.09	5 3/8	4.91	7 3/8	6.74	9 3/8	8.57
1 1/2	1.37	3 1/2	3.20	5 1/2	5.03	7 1/2	6.86	9 1/2	8.69
1 5/8	1.49	3 5/8	3.31	5 5/8	5.14	7 5/8	6.97	9 5/8	8.80
1 3/4	1.60	3 3/4	3.43	5 3/4	5.26	7 3/4	7.09	9 3/4	8.92
1 7/8	1.71	3 7/8	3.54	5 7/8	5.37	7 7/8	7.20	9 7/8	9.03
2	1.83	4	3.66	6	5.49	8	7.32	10	9.14

INDEX

HOW DO YOU SAY "THANK YOU"
TO THE ANGELS ABOVE
WHO'VE BLESSED YOUR LIFE
WITH THEIR MAGICAL LOVE.
HOW DO THEY KNOW HOW
GRATEFUL YOU ARE
FOR HAVING THEM CLOSE,
NEVER WANDERING FAR.
YOU MUST LET THEM KNOW
THAT YOU REALLY DO CARE
AND DON'T WANT THEM LIVING
JUST ANYWHERE.
GIVE THEM THIS HOUSE —
THIS HEAVENLY HOME;
GIVE THEM A PLACE
OF THEIR VERY OWN.